living in the now

Books by

FREDERIC C. WOOD Jr.

LIVING IN THE NOW

SEX AND THE NEW MORALITY

LIVING in the NOW

Spirit-Centered Faith For 20th Century Man

by Frederic C. Wood Jr.

Association Press   New York

LIVING IN THE NOW

Spirit-Centered Faith for 20th Century Man

———

Copyright © 1970 by

National Board of Young Men's Christian Associations

———

Standard Book Number: 8096–1759–5

Library of Congress Catalog Card Number: 74–93428

72

Printed in the United States of America

For Jane
A fellow learner

preface

THE ESSAYS which follow first took verbal form about four years ago. They were written down, in a quite different form from the present, and in a different order, during a leisurely summer vacation on Sanibel Island off the Gulf Coast of Florida. Since then, they have been through a number of revisions, and no small amount of rethinking.

The first stimulus came from the suggestion of a book editor that I write down some of the things I was thinking about the major religious issues of the day, particularly on a college campus. That suggestion fed into my own need and ambition to put together a more or less systematic statement of where I was theologically. I believe I envisioned a popularized theology in one volume!

Subsequent experience has persuaded me that that vision was presumptuous. I now view the collection as a series of statements, tied together by a consistent theological point of view, but eclectic rather than comprehensive in their focus. They are ad hoc elaborations of a style of life which can never be fully captured within the covers of a book.

A word about the sequence of these essays is in order. The opening chapter (which bears the title of the collection) originally came near the end. It was written after most of the other essays. But the comments of a number of readers and critics persuaded me that "living in the now" is the more central theme of the entire work. To live

7

authentically in the present tense is *the* germane dimension of the style of life presented here.

Some readers may be interested to know that the original opening essay now appears as Chapter 3. Here I am trying to deal with some of the problems of definition which underlie the whole work. This is a more academic essay. Some readers may still wish to begin there. But I am persuaded that the tone of the collection is more accurately set by the present Chapter 1.

In response to the suggestions of a number of readers, I have also appended "a personal note" to each essay. This is an attempt to be more personal and confessional with the reader by way of illustration. It is a way of putting human flesh on the bones of my theological affirmations. That seems appropriate to a collection designed to describe a style of life.

These essays have profited from the critical comments of more individuals than I can name here. Particularly helpful has been the candor of the publisher's readers, and the gentle but firm guidance of my editor, Mr. Robert A. Elfers, of Association Press. Certain parts of the manuscript were seen at various stages by colleagues and students at Goucher College and Vassar College. Their critique has been invaluable in reshaping my thinking and my modes of communicating. And thanks are due my research assistant, Miss Anita Ruhling, for patient typing, retyping, and proofreading, as well as helpful suggestions.

Finally, a book demands time and sweat, and evokes occasional anxiety and self-doubt in the author. This book has been no exception. My wife and children have suffered all of this patiently, particularly during summer vacations when most such work must be done. Better than anyone else, they know how far short I fall of the style of life I hold out here.

F. C. W. Jr.

Poughkeepsie, New York
March, 1969

When we seek to discover effective action for the church owing to the necessity for its intervention in [entering into] the world, it seems as though its first objective should be the creation of a style of life. For if we consider the life of Christians in our churches, we see certainly that they make good sons, fathers, husbands, employers, and workmen—"good, like good bread," said Aragon—they have many individual virtues, but they have no style of life, or rather, they have exactly that which has been imposed on them by their sociological conditions: that is to say, by their social class, their nation, their environment, and so on. It is not their spiritual condition which affects their style of life: it is their political or economic condition, and from this point of view, they are an overwhelming demonstration of the truth, temporary and temporal, of Marxism. Now at the present time, many Christians are fully aware that this is an intolerable situation, and that if it is allowed to go on, it will prepare the way for the total collapse of the churches of the West. This problem of the style of life is absolutely central; for it is at this point that the question of the integration of Christianity into the world, or at least of its creative power, will be most fiercely tested.

JACQUES ELLUL, *The Presence of the Kingdom*

contents

introduction

THIS BOOK IS a collection of essays. They can be read separately, but they are intended to be read together. This is because the book represents a unity of thought. As a whole, it is an attempt to set forth biblical faith, in the Judeo-Christian tradition, as a meaningful style of life for modern man. Each separate chapter focuses on one facet or expression of that style of life.

In one sense, the entire collection represents a new attempt to deal with an old question. Can religious faith be both contemporary and true to an historic tradition? The answer offered is affirmative, but only through a radical reinterpretation of the meaning of faith. This involves viewing faith as a dynamic and fluid style of life, rather than primarily as a set of beliefs, a body of moral teachings, a form of institutional allegiance, or a syndrome of religious practices. But this style of life includes all these dimensions—belief, morality, communal life, ritual practice. Consequently, specific essays deal with active expressions of faith—deciding, acting, hoping; in short, living.

In another sense, this book is a personal document. It sets forth the broad outlines of one man's faith, systematically and as unequivocally as he knows how. This faith is one response to the challenge to live with some authenticity in the twentieth century and within a Christian frame of reference.

A time of theological revolution, such as that through which we are now passing, naturally evokes such statements. Often, they add new confusion to an already confused popular theological scene. More traditional and conventional churchmen respond in dismay to what appears to be yet another erosion of the faith delivered to them. Nonbelievers and those who have been alienated from their religious traditions, on the other hand, are perplexed by those who share their doubts and concerns but still cling to what appears to them as an outmoded tradition.

I have no intention of multiplying this confusion. At the same time, I am a clergyman and a preacher who finds himself constantly challenged to say precisely what he does believe. Within an academic community, that challenge comes from a constituency particularly insistent regarding intellectual honesty. Nowhere is the demand more pressing to say what one means and mean what one says. This challenge can be addressed from the pulpit, in personal counseling, in the classroom, and in informal discussion. Still, behind what is said from the pulpit or the lectern or in informal personal contacts lies a more or less systematic theological point of view. This rarely receives elaborate treatment in any of the media in which a college chaplain communicates. It is this point of view for which students and colleagues probe with refreshingly incessant questioning of theological ideas, their logical and experiential bases, their relationship to normative documents and tradition, and, above all, their relevance to life amid the complexities of twentieth-century society.

A nonreligious student activist says bluntly: "I'd like to know how you're grounded." Another student writes simply but with passion: "Please tell me about your God." An elderly churchwoman comments: "I'm clear about what you don't believe, but not so sure what you believe in. What holds you together?" In articulating such a faith, one must begin by acknowledging that it is in a constant state of flux. No one formulation remains eternally valid, even for one individual. And no one formulation retains the same meaning for one individual over any extended period of time. The statement that "God is love," for example, has a changing content as the experience of an individual expands. Is it then worthwhile to attempt a statement of faith which will be outdated even by the author's experience in a short time?

The attempt seems justified on several grounds. First, there is a constancy in the midst of flux for any faith which identifies itself with a particular tradition. This is partly due to the hardy resilience of theological language, which tends to survive periodic attacks on its relevance.

Second, there is a subtle interrelationship between experience and perception. One's perceptions are deeply informed by the frame of reference he brings to his experience, even though any experience may alter one's view of himself and his world. Consequently, a man's faith is itself the ground out of which changes in his faith will come.

Third, those to whom this book is addressed are entitled to clear, candid statements, even within the limitations of relativity and flux. Without such statements, theological communication atrophies.[1] A living faith requires what has come to be called theological encounter and dialogue. This book is dedicated to the proposition that all men are entitled to statements which are as unambiguous as possible in this area, particularly from those of us who use theological language and assume the role of theological interpreters.

If each age requires new formulations of old theological truths, then it is the task of those who hold to those old truths to provide the new formulations. This is true regardless of how tentative, quickly dated, or relative the new formulation may be. Lowell is right that

> New occasions teach new duties,
> Time makes ancient good uncouth.
> They must upward still and onward
> Who would keep abreast of truth.[2]

Such reformulation is, after all, the task of theology. Present trends toward popularization are rescuing theology from a state in which theological work was being written by professionals for professionals. The result, at least in the American Church, was that most of the exciting theological ideas of the past four decades were kept safely locked within the walls of academia. The Church at large meanwhile continued to perceive herself and the world in terms which became increasingly out of touch with life, as well as with the traditions which the Church and her theology purport to preserve.

This means that, at yet another level, these essays reflect an attempt to set forth a "new" theological perspective. The word *new* needs to be used advisedly here, since what is said is deeply influenced by other currents of modern thought, both secular and religious. My perspective is also decidedly not new insofar as it is grounded in both the Bible and the history of Christian thought. However, in the relative sense that it conflicts with much of what prevails and passes for orthodoxy in the Church today, the central thesis of the book is new. This is that the key to biblical faith is an understanding of God as spirit. Likewise, the key to recapturing an authentically Christian style of life for our time is the priority of the Spirit over any and all religious forms delivered to us. These are the forms of belief, behavior, ritual, and communal life in which the Spirit men call God has at particular times and places been understood to "reside." A recurrent motif in the essays which follow is that all such forms stand under the judgment of the Spirit which they serve. In its name they may need to be discarded or at least radically redefined in our time. All of this points to the need for what I have called a "spirit-centered" theology. What the book is all about then is a spirit-centered style of life.

To whom, then, is this book addressed? At first glance, it would appear, to the household of faith. Such folk share many of my presuppositions, including the normative nature of the biblical narrative. But that answer is oversimplified and inadequate. There are many with whom one can today carry on a meaningful theological dialogue without common assumptions concerning the Christian tradition and the Bible. Consequently, I prefer to address this book to my fellow pilgrims—to all who are struggling with the meaning and purpose of their life, the basis for their decision making, and the nature of their ultimate commitments. These are the real existential questions around which my own pilgrimage in faith continues to focus. I find them often raised by persons of active mind who live more or less on the fringe of the Church. They are questions which seem to be particularly acute for college students. Perhaps, more than to any other single group, this book is addressed to them.

The reader will find little that is new or original in these pages. Neither will he find an exhaustive treatment of theological issues. The issues dealt with in the six chapters are not developed in all of their nuances, and certainly the book does not cover the whole gamut of contemporary theological concern. I have instead focused on those areas in which I find people to be most concerned, involved, or perplexed.

The opening chapter treats a question rarely discussed in the popular theological literature of our time. Strangely, it is a question central to my own faith. It is also one which I find to be of concern to many honestly inquiring people. This is the question of eternal life. What does a modern Christian mean by this idea? And what does he *not* mean? What role does this affirmation play in the life style we call faith?

Next I discuss the relationship between faith and ethics, commitment and decision making. This is not only an area of special concern in a time of rapid social change and moral upheaval. It is also *the* area in which traditional Christian religion has seemed to be most out of touch with itself and, for many, most meaningless—if not hypocritical. A fresh approach to the meaning of faith requires a new morality, one by which an individual makes his own decisions on the basis of his own internalized ideals.

There follows a discussion of the relationship of faith to belief. There is great confusion today, particularly among young people, between intellectual assent to doctrine and personal response and commitment to an idea or value. Many are hung up on the difference between faith and religion, mistakenly assuming you must be a religious believer to be a man of faith.

Questions of belief lead into the next chapter on the relationship between faith and the religious establishment. This raises some of the problems involved in being individually committed while maintaining a meaningful relationship to a community of common commitment. This is particularly a problem for the younger clergy today, although it has really always been a problem for anyone who strives to be an honest man of faith.

Dealing with the Church raises related questions of the relationship of faith to religious practices. How does a modern man worship and pray? How can he maintain the integrity of a faith expressed in words that are not his own? What is the place of discipline in a time when much traditional religious discipline seems discredited or antiquated.

The book closes with an attempt to rearticulate the biblical hope in a modern world. This is a "Where do we go from here?" chapter. It is appropriate that it comes at the end, particularly as a "theology of hope" is emerging as the latest in a series of recent theological developments. This chapter presupposes everything else in the book, and at the same time undergirds it. It says, in brief, why faith is an exciting and rewarding *modus vivendi*.

Some may be concerned that I have paid the price of relevance in order to keep myself in touch with a particular tradition. Others may fear that I have sacrificed my biblical Judeo-Christian roots in an effort to be both contemporary and relevant. With such readers I feel deep sympathy and rapport. In some ways they represent two warring sides of my own being.[3] But I can finally only respond to them that this style of life is for me both relevant and traditional. It is the faith delivered to me as I perceive it in my time.

1

living in the now

MOST WHO SEEK a meaningful faith or life-style today are ultimately concerned with living authentically in the present tense. They seek to become fuller persons. Or they hope to realize their human potential. Or they simply want to feel more "real."

Whatever the euphemism, the emphasis is on living in the now. Not yesterday's memories; not tomorrow's promises; but today: Let me be, and be fully. That is the plea of modern man. And it has a great deal to do with the faith around which he can fashion an authentic style of life.

But living in the now is dependent on some sense of that under which the present moment always stands. Let us call it the "morethan-now." It is what has been classically understood as the eternal. Hence, this statement of a modern, here-and-now-oriented style of life begins at the unlikely point of discussing the relationship between faith and eternal life. This is required since the capacity to live in the now is the first and most important earmark of faith's style of life.

But, is the nature of the eternal really a burning issue today? Certainly it has not been a prominent topic of discussion in most recent theological literature. Indeed, systematic treatment of eternal life is conspicuously absent from the popularized theology of our time. One suspects that theologians either take it for granted or avoid it because it is embarrassing.

However, misinformation and confusion in this area constitute a serious intellectual stumbling block for many thoughtful people. Probably in no other realm of Christian thought has theology been so fogged over with an aura of magic and naïve supernaturalism. In general, the time-transcending dimension of faith has been either ignored or presented in a way which violates the intellectual integrity of twentieth-century man. The choice offered has usually been between "life under death" and "life after death." The first option asserts that death casts a shadow of meaninglessness over even the most meaningful experiences of life.[1] The second holds that death is a mirage because of the gift of a new life which extends in time and space from the point of death. Neither option has very much to do with biblical faith. The first often sees itself as a reaction to that faith, and the second often presents itself as the orthodox expression of faith. This confusion should be dispelled. Another classical alternative is available and needs articulation in our time.

Moreover, a proper understanding of the eternal dimension of faith provides the linchpin for a theology in which God is understood primarily as Spirit. Spirit-centered faith stands or falls on the *eternal* nature of its God. For example, where God is identified as the spirit of Love, faith affirms a time-transcending quality to Love. It is before and beyond and behind all things. (This is how the concept of the eternal *Logos* (Word) is used in John's Gospel. The central affirmation of that Gospel is that in the person of Jesus the Logos "became flesh" (John 1:14), i.e., was revealed in the form of a man.) Love transcends the limits of the existence of any particular "lover." Also, a spirit-centered theology points to the proper meaning of eternal life because it insists on a distinction between spirit and form. This allows one to reject the form of life after death while affirming the eternal quality of the spirit. And faith responding to an eternal spirit represents actual participation in the eternal . . . now.

Another reason for concern with eternal life is that it holds the key to the biblical understanding of time. The Bible is marked by a very specific view of history (measured time) and its purpose. The purpose of history is to point beyond itself. And what lies beyond history is the eternal, that for which there is neither beginning nor end, that which is both alpha and omega. This imagery of beginning and end is used to describe Jesus in Rev. 1:8. It also sheds light on certain cryptic temporal sayings ascribed to him, e.g., "Before Abraham was, I am" (John 8:58).

Also, some grasp of eternal life is a presupposition of each essay that follows, culminating in a valid hope for man today. Some, indeed, hold that the biblical hope *is* eternal life and that any separation of the two confuses the issue. There is an element of truth in this insofar as hope is inseparable from faith. But hope becomes either romanticized or unreal when the eternal dimension of faith is not properly understood. Among other things, this requires a rethinking of basic psychological and theological concepts.

THE UNITY OF BODY AND SOUL

One such concept shared by psychology and theology is the *body*. Psychologists and theologians today tend to agree in assuming a relationship between one's body and one's identity. Indeed, they recognize that one does not have an identity without a body. One's body is a fundamental determinant of his selfhood. In a real sense, you are your body.

But what is selfhood? What does it mean to say that one is or has a self? What does "identity" really designate? Are these simply meaningless abstractions in an age which thinks in quantifiable terms? Or do they refer to a reality of human experience? [2] Certainly, they all refer to a personal spirit. They point to that which is uniquely me or you. They designate that intangible reality, "me," of which one's body is the outward and visible sign. This self is presupposed by every thought and experience one has. Every perception is of that which stands in some relationship to the "me," one's self. This is not to say that the self can be objectified and quantified or that it refers to some little man or homunculus who lives inside the body. [3] It affirms only that one dimension of human experience is one's uniqueness, one's self, one's identity, one's personhood.

This self is presupposed by most meaningful discourse. It is very difficult to communicate, for example, through the pages of this book, without some assumption that human spirit is speaking to human spirit. In writing, I assume that which is uniquely and irreducibly "me" and that which is uniquely and irreducibly "you." The same reality is designated biblically and theologically as *soul*. Indeed, the New Testament word for soul, *psyche,* should be translated "self."

It is the root of that discipline which investigates the nature of the intangible self, i.e., psychology.[4] And in the jargon of the American black community, "soul" has come to refer to a sense of identity. The black man who has soul is one who knows and embraces who he is, including his blackness.

In both the Old and New Testaments, a man's soul represents his uniqueness. The Hebrew word in the Old Testament is *nephesh,* and it is clear that every man has his own *nephesh.* It is also inextricably wedded to his body. It is not some discrete organ which can be located by surgery. Neither is it a discrete function or entity which can be separated from its body. In the Bible, there are no disembodied souls and there are no dis-souled bodies. In the Hebraic understanding, when a man dies his soul (self, psyche, identity) does not depart from his body. It simply becomes inert, inactive, weak, powerless, devitalized. The life flows out of it, usually under the image of blood. The body becomes disorganized, but it is still a body/soul.[5] Hence, the pervasive Hebraic reverence for dead bodies. They continue to be the outward and visible signs of souls. Therefore one does not desecrate them. (See, for example, the reaction of the relatives of Saul to the desecration of his body, I Sa. 31:8–13.) Objectified, such an understanding becomes absurd. A dead body is a dead body. To act as if it continued to be the habitation of some living entity called a soul is to invite magical thinking. But subjectively viewed, this understanding of the relationship between soul and body after death is psychologically sound. Imagine the difference between your reaction to an anonymous corpse and the corpse of someone close. Yet both are "simply" dead bodies.

If the unity of body and soul is biblical, why is it not more widely accepted within those traditions which claim to be grounded in the Bible? Partly because the Bible itself is ambiguous on this subject. And it becomes more so in the later writings as the influence of Greek thought becomes more pervasive. The Old Testament maintains a reasonably consistent unitarian view of the relationship of body and soul. In the New Testament, the Greek dualism which makes the body of secondary importance begins to manifest itself. This is particularly clear in the Pauline distinction between spirit and flesh.[6] This dualism leads to the doctrine of the immortality of a disembodied soul, an idea often confused with the biblical understanding of resurrection. Even the contexts in which Paul makes his spirit/flesh dichotomy have more to do with Paul's mode of moral exhortation than with any ultimate division of body and soul beyond the grave.

A second reason for body/soul dualism in popular religious thought is that the Church maintains a distinction between spirit and form. This distinction lies at the heart of the Christian sacramental view of the world. The problem with applying it to human nature is that in the process, the distinction becomes "desacramentalized." This is particularly clear in belief in life after death. When one desacramentalizes the spirit/form polarity, one comes to believe that spirit can be experienced without form. This is the opposite of idolatry, which desacramentalizes the spirit/form unity by assuming that a form can have ultimate significance without the "indwelling" of its spirit.

The most telling attack on the desacramentalization of human nature in our time has come not from biblical theologians but from psychologists. Their primary concern is the systematic exploration of the human psyche. Particularly as they have emerged under the heading of "holistic" psychology, these explorations point to the unity of man's self/soul and his body.[7] The emergence of psychosomatic medicine points to the same truth. Man can make a division between his self and his body only at the peril of the health of both. Health is, after all, the total health of a body/soul.[8] Such a holistic view sheds light on biblical accounts of faith healing. These are often objectified in popular lore in ways that can lead only to magical thinking and medical quackery. But faith healing is neither magic nor crazy when one assumes that self and body are so wedded that one can speak of their health (wholeness) only in terms of their unity.

One of the ironies of recent theological thought is that a movement in the Christian tradition to reassert this unity has become instead an instrument for maintaining Greek dualism under Christian labels. This is Christian Science, which has its roots in therapeutic evidence for the unity of body and soul. Like most schismatic movements in the history of the Church, Christian Science was inevitable in order to call the Church back to a fuller understanding of her ministry. One of the effects of that ministry is the healing of soul/ bodies. Christian Science recognizes this. However, Christian Science doctrine denies the underlying unity, and finally denies the reality of the body. This is desacramentalization. It leads not only to the worship of an amorphous spirit (i.e., a spirit without a medium). It also leads to sometimes tragic expressions of a misplaced faith.

Belief in body-soul unity is also at the heart of biblical insistence on the resurrection of the *body* as opposed to the immortality of the *soul.* The resurrection of the body is not simply an emphasis on form to the neglect of spirit, however. Nor is it belief in resuscitated corpses, in spite of the metaphorical use of just this image in some biblical accounts.[9] The resurrection of the body instead includes both form and spirit. It is a recognition that spirit cannot endure in time without form. It says that if the spirit of Christ is eternal, if it endures in time beyond the existence of the man Jesus, it must endure in some form. The concern of the Christian then is not with resurrected bodies, i.e., people who have been raised from the dead, revitalized forms. The concern of the Christian is to search out and recognize that form under which his eternal spirit is now revealed, in which "He" now dwells. This is the insight behind the classical understanding of the Church as the Body of Christ.[10] It is the corporate form which the Love/spirit takes in history subsequent to the destruction of Jesus' form (the Crucifixion). The good news of the Resurrection has nothing to do with a resuscitated corpse. It has to do with the fact that the spirit lives. "He" is risen! It is good news because the worst possible news, that the form of the spirit has been destroyed, is overcome in the recognition that the spirit itself could not be killed. "He" endures in spite of the fate of any and all forms. The sequence of Crucifixion–Resurrection means that every form must die in order for the spirit to be set free. This keeps the form itself from becoming an object of idolatry. And therein lies the most radical expression of the prophetic spirit of biblical faith. All forms must eventually die in order to set the spirit free.

LIFE AFTER DEATH

The popular belief in life after death is then both unbiblical and inconsistent with a Christian faith-response. It is also idolatrous because it makes the conditioned (existence) unconditional (eternal). This popular belief is that there is available to men a self-conscious existence in time and/or space after death. Our age requires explicit rejection of this idea because it is so deeply embedded in the fabric of contemporary faith and practice. It is reflected in most Christian funeral liturgies and other formal prayers. For example, in the Episcopal *Book of Common Prayer,* we pray for the "continual growth" of the dead (p. 75). Likewise, the Order for the Burial of the Dead includes the prayer that the deceased may increase "in knowledge and love" (p. 332). Language concerning one's life "beyond the grave" has become a form of religious jargon. Some form of this belief is probably accepted by the majority of churchgoers, as well as by others who are not meaningfully related to organized religion. It is even clung to by many Jews (who should know better!).

Why the apparent tenacity of this belief? Perhaps because the biblical view of life and history is harsh. It makes demands on man. A faith which makes one responsible *now* to serve the eternal spirit is discomforting. The imperative to find ultimate meaning here and now is hard to accept. If this "vale of tears" is really all there is, one might be tempted to give up the struggle of living. Perhaps we need to believe there are cookies at the end of the rainbow, even when we suspect they are a mirage. Perhaps the moral responsibility of not being able to postpone fellowship with one's God is too great to accept. Perhaps the burden of living in the reality of the present, rather than the illusion of the future, is too heavy for most men.

If such escapism underlies the tenacity of belief in life after death, then it is not only un-Christian, it is anti-Christian. It is not only inappropriate to the Christian faith-response; it is antagonistic. It tempts men away from the realm of real history. According to the biblical view, history is the realm of the activity of God. The man of faith finds himself called to participate in this activity. Any escape route from history should therefore be suspect. (In *The Autobiography of Malcolm X* [11] one reason that the author sees Christianity as the white devil's religion is that its pie-in-the-sky promises have been used to dupe the black man and keep him in his social place.) With its objectified images of heaven or nirvana, a kind of carefree existence beyond existence, belief in life after death can be both intellectually unrespectable and morally irresponsible.

Consequently, along with the existence of God, this doctrine requires a frontal assault from the spirit-centered theologian. It calls for explicit rejection because it is inconsistent with a spirit-centered understanding of reality, because it is intellectually untenable for large numbers of modern men, and because it can be morally debilitating.[12]

A DYNAMIC UNDERSTANDING OF RESURRECTION

In place of a new existence beyond the grave, spirit-centered theology suggests a dynamic understanding of the resurrection. This is present-oriented, morally demanding, and nonillusory. It has been "demagicalized" and can be confirmed in the data of everyday experience. Here the resurrection is interpreted sacramentally, as an outward and visible sign of the ongoing life of the Spirit.

Such an understanding is dynamic because it views the resurrection event as something which *happens* in one's life today, rather than something which once happened to someone else or will happen to me. Resurrection refers to present time. It has to do with the Love of Christ impinging on one's life and working through him in his time and place. To say that the resurrection is central to Christian faith is not to say that faith depends on a man being miraculously raised from the dead two thousand years ago. That is probably a very undynamic belief, for those who hold it. It is like the belief that dinosaurs once roamed the earth—interesting but not powerfully related to the here and now. Neither does the importance of the resurrection hang on the hope that one will self-consciously survive his own death. For some, that might be a dynamic hope, insofar as their existence is experienced as meaningless. For others, for whom resurrection means that the present has been given an eternal meaning, such a hope is unappetizing.

A dynamic, present-oriented grasp of resurrection focuses on the reality of the Spirit now. It is the only understanding of resurrection which is consistent with a spirit-centered theology. In spite of the prevalence of past- and future-oriented interpretations of the resurrection within the Church, an orientation to the present is most consistent with the celebration of the Easter event. Easter worship begins with the triumphant announcement *He is risen!* Christians do not say "He rose." Neither do they say "You will rise." Neither of those statements conveys the heart of the Easter "good news." The past-oriented statement objectifies a myth, and the future-oriented statement holds out false promises. The heart of the Easter message is that the God who is spirit is alive among us at this moment. The New Testament Greek proclamation is "He has risen," present perfect. This too proclaims a *present* reality. "He" survives all the buffetings of history and the unloving proclivities of men, for which the Crucifixion stands as an historical symbol. This is good news because it reassures one that in spite of the "Crucifixion-experience" of his existence, the Love to which he strives to give himself cannot be destroyed. And it offers an opportunity to continue participating in that which is eternal—the love of God experienced as spirit.

This view gives a clue to the meaning of the "real presence" of Christ. Those who objectify this metaphor (for example, in the sacrament of the Mass) miss its point and reduce its power. They translate it into the kind of "spiritualism" and communication with departed persons which is considered pagan in Holy Scripture! [13] The "real presence" of Christ refers to the experience of his spirit as a present reality. This "presence" is not limited to formal worship, although it is traditionally identified with certain ritual acts. This is because they represent occasions when the self-consciousness of faith should be heightened and the members of the community are in one another's presence. In spite of abuse of the "real presence" in much Roman Catholic thought and its nonuse in much Protestant thought, a spirit-centered theology stands or falls on the validity of this doctrine. It presupposes the experience of the Spirit as a present reality.

What form then does this Spirit take when it is encountered in the present? It is certainly not limited to a particular form, and it may take any form. Most often it takes the form of another person. This is because, within the Christian faith-response, the normative form is a person. The Christian God/spirit consequently has an irreducibly personal nature. Therefore, one can experience the real presence of Christ in an act of self-giving service by another person. That person in that moment becomes Christ for one. In him is experienced the "real presence" of the spirit which was in Jesus and which could not be crucified. The other person becomes an illustration of "Christ incognito." This is the experience of the Emmaus Road story [14] in which two people (who knew Jesus) encounter a stranger who ministers to their needs. Only subsequently do they realize that this indeed was the risen Christ. That does not mean that Jesus was walking around in a clever disguise. It means that the Christ-spirit is encountered in another. The resurrection becomes at that moment a living reality. And appropriately, the disciples hurry off to share this "good news" with others. Their sharing entails not only a verbal report but also their "being Christ" to others. There, in its simplicity and profundity, is the meaning of Christian ministry. It is a response to the call to be Christ to one another. And through such ministry, the resurrection is perpetuated. The Spirit lives on in new forms. And endless generations repeat the good news that "He" is indeed risen—now, in our time.

Only by accepting an infinite variety of forms for its Spirit can the Church speak of itself as the Body of Christ. At one level, that is a presumptuous statement; and the Church itself often puts the lie to it. But at another level, to call the Church the Body of Christ is like calling Israel the people of God. The metaphor points to the community's self-understanding as an outward and visible form which perpetuates the Christ-spirit down through history. The historical existence of the Church is not a "proof" of the resurrection in the empirical sense, since the Church at a given moment may be devoid of the Spirit. But the ongoing life of a community of faith, an invisible Church, does document the resurrection. It is the real Body of Christ. It is the ever-changing but ever-same "new" form which his spirit assumes.

What then of the initial resurrection event? Sooner or later, every serious Christian asks himself: "But what do you think *really* happened on the first Easter morning?" A spirit-centered theology which interprets resurrection mythologically is still bound to come to grips with this question. However, its answer will not be based on the questionable historical data, but rather on the experience of the resurrection as a present reality. Present experience is then projected into the past. We all do this, whether or not historians consider it methodologically respectable. Just as the present is understood in the light of the past, so too our interpretation of the past is influenced by present experience. The details of faith's projection are subject to all of the tentativeness of any historical hypothesis. But its substance reflects the nature of the present experience on which faith itself is based.

What then might have happened that would be consistent with present experience and reconcilable with biblical accounts? Might not Jesus' followers have had an experience *in community* which persuaded them that the Spirit they had detected in him was alive among *them?* Indeed, not only this, but the power of his spirit had been transmitted to them as the new mediators. This would make their community the new form of that Spirit. We have no idea how this recognition came to them beyond the way it comes to us, which is usually through the ministry of another person. Perhaps it came through their ministry to one another, even amid the confusion and depression which set in after Friday afternoon. The Emmaus Road story and the account of the gift of the Spirit suggest such an experience.[15]

To propose this is, of course, to be selective in one's reading of Scripture. But any dynamic faith which reconstructs the past through the eyes of the present cannot avoid this selectivity. And it does not make other resurrection accounts necessarily meaningless. Indeed, some of them can have great power and meaning when they are interpreted metaphorically and mythologically. Selectivity does, however, give some biblical accounts greater historical weight than others. No one but the most rigid biblical literalist avoids this.

Focusing on Acts 2 may suggest an inadequate distinction between resurrection and inspiration, between Easter and Whitsunday. Such distinctions are helpful for pedagogical purposes, but experientially Whitsunday has as much to do with Easter as does Christmas or any other celebration of the faith. A spirit-bearing community has as much to do with the return of the Spirit in a new form as the Incarnation has to do with the experience of a spirit-bearing person in the present.

A focus on the Emmaus Road and pentecostal narratives, however, does lend less historical weight to other resurrection accounts in the New Testament. Stories of dead people who walk through doors and have fingers poked into their sides,[16] who carefully fold their shrouds before going visiting, who leave angelic messengers to report on them,[17] who are bodily whisked away into the sky,[18] are so foreign to our experience of the real world (and of the spirit of Christ!) as to be quite incredible as historical accounts. Such stories can have meaning, however, when viewed as attempts by the early Church to put its message in communicable narrative form and to meet the response of skeptics.

This attitude also applies to biblical accounts of an empty tomb.[19] These are the favorites of the believers in life after death and "resuscitated corpse" theories of the resurrection. (Canon Lloyd, who elsewhere appears sympathetic to radical theology, faults Bishop Robinson in his treatment of miracles in *Honest to God* for not mentioning "the supreme miracle of the Empty Tomb.")[20] For a spirit-centered theology, the historicity of the empty tomb is preposterous

... unless, as some have suggested, it was a trick! Indeed, if it were possible to demonstrate the historicity of the empty tomb through a photographic record, faith in Jesus as *the* medium of the Spirit would be badly shaken. He would become either a superman or a charlatan. Since we are not supermen and charlatanism contradicts faith's image of Jesus, this would present difficulties for a Christian faith-response.

A dynamic understanding of the resurrection is also more meaningful morally than is a focus on the past or the future. One is called here and now to be a mediator of his God. A present-oriented grasp of resurrection will not allow escape from the moral demands of faith. Strangely, some cling to belief in life after death as a basis for Christian morality. They fear that without this promise the incentive for "good" behavior is removed. But this perverts morality. It becomes then simply manipulative decision making, designed to obtain maximum rewards. In addition to its negative estimate of human nature (we will only do the good for a future reward), such thinking undercuts the basis of Christian morality as a response to Love.

ETERNITY NOW!

Since eternal life is still understood as a gift to those who love in response to Christ, it needs redefinition. Within a spirit-centered theology, eternal life is *eternity now*. It is my participation in that which is eternal in the here and now. The relationship of eternal life to faith is that in faith one perceives himself to be "in touch" with that Spirit which transcends time. And if his faith is dynamic, he actively participates in that Spirit. One tastes eternity. The proper tense for Christian affirmations concerning eternal life is present perfect, not future. The good news is that I *have been* given eternal life, not that *I will be* given it.

In words attributed to Jesus, "the hour comes" but it also "now is." [21] To say that the "hour comes" is to say that faith carries the promise of ever-new possibilities for participation in the Spirit in one's lifetime. It says nothing about what will happen after death. Its future orientation simply recognizes the unfulfilled nature of Christian faith. This is Kierkegaard's understanding that Christians are always in a process of "becoming." [22] "And now is" means that we know this because the hour has already arrived. Eternity is available now. Therefore it is also a promise for the future. This is what

it means to say that the Kingdom of Heaven is upon us. It is why
John the Baptist allegedly announces that it is "at hand," [23] and why
Jesus can proclaim that it is a *fait accompli*.[24] But the experience of
the kingdom in the present always points to its promise for the future,
its ever-new "becoming." St. Paul speaks of *having* the Spirit "in
earnest," [25] which means as a down payment. Because of what the
man of faith perceives himself to have received, he knows there is
more to come. But, paradoxically, what he has received is experienced as the fullness of the eternal spirit. It is eternity now.

There is an analogy to this in marriage. In a good marriage relationship one believes he is experiencing the fullness of love. The
truth of that judgment is not demonstrable to others. The only two
people who can make it are the marriage partners. If anyone told
them that they were wrong, that they were "missing out" on something important, they would not believe it because of their experience of one another. At the same time, such a relationship always
holds promise for the future. It promises future fulfillments which
lovers anticipate. One of the bases for this is past experience which
tells them that their relationship is in a constant state of becoming.
Like the relationship between man and his God, it is never static.
The hour of fulfillment is always coming, but one only knows that
because it has already arrived. And the future promise of marriage
is within one's lifetime, not beyond the grave. Likewise with the paradox of eternity as a promise, but also now.

What are the implications of this view for an attitude toward
death? How can the man of faith say that the sting of death has
been removed or that death has been overcome? [26] For many, these
affirmations lie at the heart of faith's good news. For a spirit-centered
theology, such affirmations are also central. But their meaning lies
in a subjective, not an objective interpretation. To say that in faith
death has been overcome is not to say that one will not die. Neither
is it to say that death is an illusion because we have been promised
a new existence later on. It is rather to say that because one participates in the eternal now, his death does not make any essential difference. Nothing, including death, can take this participation away
from him. In Paul's terms, nothing can separate one from the love of
God.[27] Therefore, nothing can deprive him of the eternity he already
has. What should be of great concern to us is not death, but life. And
what is of concern about life is not its quantity, but its quality. A

Christian measures that quality by the integrity of his response to the eternal Spirit. Hence, the ultimate judgment of one's life is already beyond the conditions of time. Insofar as one participates in that Love which is eternal, that which always was and always will be, he is eternal and his death is overcome.

Such thinking provides the rationale for Christian martyrdom. Martyrdom says: Because the quality of my life is more important than its quantity, the integrity of my response to God is more important than my life. Part of the Gospel's promise is that through such acts the Love/spirit is reborn in the personhood of another. The confident self-giving of one's life is shaking to the man who does not share your faith. When this man is your persecutor, submission confronts him with a reality of which he was unaware. He is confronted with a new kind of power. This insight is at the root of biblical injunctions to turn the other cheek, to walk the extra mile, and to love one's enemies. These injunctions are strategic as well as expressive of the Love/spirit. They make submission in faith a form of witness. They point toward the "shaking up" of the enemy in the name of Love. This presupposes the enemy's full humanity and his capacity to respond to the Love/spirit. And it is why nonviolent resistance can be so powerful, politically as well as "spiritually." It explains Gandhi's confidence, incomprehensible to many of his compatriots, in the capacity of his British persecutors to be changed by Love. Dietrich Bonhoeffer, probably *the* Christian martyr of the twentieth century, reportedly converted his Nazi prison guards by the quality of his relationship to them. Such loving of one's enemies is empowered by the faith that the love survives—even one's own death. It gives the courage for authentic living in the now. Another "now liver" of the present generation was Martin Luther King—significantly also a martyr, one for whom fulfillment in the present was more important than promises for the future.

The biblical understanding of time, then, is that it always "stands under" eternity. Biblically, time is viewed *sub specie aeternitas*. The function of history is to point beyond itself. It is to point to that Spirit which makes history "tick." Therefore, the function of faithful acts within history is to point to this Spirit. This is done by making the Spirit real within history, by acting it out, by "realizing" it. That is the vocation of man according to the biblical view: to act out the Spirit in the realm of history. It is why "service" should always be the first word when Christians and Jews discuss their common calling. The "suffering servant" passages in Isaiah 40–55 refer to the vocation of the people of Israel as well as to the ministry acted out by Jesus. Indeed, the ministry of Jesus represents a focusing of the vocation of Israel in one man. This is primarily service of the biblical God/spirit. But because that Spirit is personal, because it is identified as Love, this service will also be service of one's fellow man. That is why love of God and love of neighbor in the Bible finally mean the same thing. They cannot be separated.[28]

It is through both giving and receiving such service that the man of faith participates in the eternal spirit and sees himself as receiving the gift of eternal life. Hence, eternal life is inextricable from biblical faith. It is also inextricable from the present time. It is the gift which releases one from fear to live in the now.

A PERSONAL NOTE

Because the eternal nature of Love is so central to the author's faith, the best illustration of this view of eternity will be personal.

In discussions of this subject, I am frequently asked three personal questions. They come as often from those who are attracted by my point of view as from those who are repelled by it. These questions are: (1) How do you feel about your own death? Are you frightened by it? Don't you at least hope there is something beyond? (2) How do you react to the death of those you love? (3) How do you hope others will respond to your death? How would you like it to be celebrated, "handled," or interpreted?

To the first question I answer that the exact time of my death is less important than the quality of my life. I hope that I shall always behave accordingly. But, of course, I do have anxieties about death. I would ordinarily prefer to extend my lifespan and usually take every precaution to do so. I still grit my teeth when my airplane takes off and lands, and I still go to the doctor when I think that my health is in peril. I think this is a healthy expression of my humanity. It means that I find life in general enjoyable. I recognize in it the promise of ever-new opportunities for participation in the spirit which for me is ultimate. Therefore, I *am* "frightened" by the prospect of my death and by the mystery of the experience itself. But I hope that this fear will never interfere with my service of my God. That is the crucial point.

As for the possibility that there "might" be something beyond, I do not cherish such a hope. This is partly because I think it undercuts a full response to the Spirit in the here and now, partly because I do not find the prospect of a new existence particularly appealing.

Second, as far as I am aware, I respond to the death of those I know with sorrow that a meaningful relationship has been terminated. This sorrow is usually marked by some self-pity over my loss and some guilt over my involvement in the relationship. An elaboration of these feelings is not within the scope of the present work. What is more important for faith is that I respond to the death of others with some joy and celebration of their life. When I have had a meaningful relationship with a person, his death represents the end of something meaningful. It directs my attention to the meaning which the relationship held for me. Death directs one's attention to the spirit to which another was a witness. I feel joy in the life of that spirit, and in the conviction that it is not dying with this person. This is why every Christian funeral service should be an opportunity to celebrate the resurrection, although most funeral liturgies make this celebration difficult. When the resurrection is celebrated, one is remembering the resurrection of Christ as a model for what has been revealed in the life of this particular person. One is not celebrating a *personal* resurrection of this individual's soul, spirit, or body to a new existence in time and space. One simply celebrates that this person tasted eternity while he was here and was the salt of the life of others so that they also tasted it through him.

This indicates what I hope for in the response of others to my death. I hope that they will use my death as an occasion to celebrate my life. And I hope they will be clear that they are celebrating the resurrection of the Spirit to "whom" I have tried to devote my life. I hope that at my funeral service there will be lusty singing of my favorite Easter hymns and good fellowship. People should celebrate the Spirit to which my life, I hope, has pointed. I also hope that it will be a family occasion, and that everyone will have a good party and perhaps get a little bit drunk. I know that there will be tears, and that does not disturb me. Tears go hand-in-hand with the kind of celebration I have in mind. I hope they will be expressive of genuine personal involvement. I know that my wife will feel sorrow over her "loss." I think that is appropriate. I hope she will be comforted in her sorrow by those who understand. That comfort should not consist of attempts to persuade her that she has not suffered a loss. She has. Above all, I hope that the whole occasion will not be marred by any talk about my "living on" beyond my death. That, I think, would be very sad. It would not only hold out an illusion, but it could get in the way of a real celebration of the living Spirit. This means that the funeral liturgy will have to be somewhat unorthodox by present standards. But that too would be appropriate for a life which has celebrated the orthodoxy of the apparently unorthodox in the name of the Spirit.

My wife and I have agreed that the conditions outlined hold for both our funerals. We have also agreed that we would like our bodies given for whatever scientific purpose they can serve. That seems not only a good way of beating the exorbitant fees of the undertaker, but also a final act of giving our body/souls for the benefit of our fellow man.

deciding for yourself

HOW HE BEHAVES is one important way a man shows his faith. The decisions one makes and the values which govern these decisions express a style of life. This has traditionally been viewed as the realm of ethics or moral theology. And ethics and morality, problems of value and decision making, have always been a central concern of theology.

Consequently, a faith which is a relevant style of life must include a relevant morality. If our morality is our style of decision making, then it should include a process or a form which defines responsible decision making. The relationship between faith and ethics lies in this that any theory of decision making finally makes appeal to an ultimate value. This is true even of so-called "ethical relativism," which eschews absolute values, but then introduces at least one such value as a hidden agenda. An avowed relativist who says: "There are no absolutes. I decide what is good in a given situation depending on the situation and the consequences," is really saying: "There are no absolute rules." The question he must now answer is: On what basis (absolute!) do you determine that a particular form of behavior is good in one situation, not good in another? [1]

The relationship between faith and morality then has to do with the ultimate nature of both. Faith is response to what one perceives to be ultimate. Ethics represent the expression (in concrete actions and decisions) of an ultimate value. There is no such thing as a

viable and consistent ethic without some form of faith. Likewise, faith
remains a dead letter until it expresses itself in decisions.[2]

The words "ethical" and "moral" will be used interchangeably
here. They are not synonymous with good as opposed to bad (as
when one says that he has made a *moral* decision and means that
he has made a *good* decision). *Ethical* and *moral* are descriptive
terms. They refer to any decision which appeals to a self-conscious
value (e.g., love, kindness) or to some concrete code.

What kind of morality might then characterize a spirit-centered
faith? What is a meaningful Christian morality for our time? Traditionally, answers to this question have focused on the form of decisions and behavior. Appeal is made to absolute forms of behavior
(e.g., it is good to honor your father and mother) with little attention paid to the process by which decisions are made. In such thinking (e.g., legalism with its appeal to absolute rules or casuistry with
its appeal to normative "case studies"), it is assumed that the form
of "good" behavior is absolute while the process through which one
arrives at a "good" decision is relative to a number of factors. These
include historical and cultural context and one's social and/or
physiological maturity. In our time, however, there has re-emerged
in the Christian tradition a type of moral thinking which tends to
be more relativistic about the form of behavior and more absolutistic
about the process of decision making.

Such a "relativistic" morality is more compatible with a faith
which is seen as a life-style and which is relativistic about the forms
of its belief. Indeed, such a "new" morality is a direct expression of
the subjectivism and relativism involved in living authentically in
the now. A life-style focused on the process of one's response more
than on its form will naturally lead to an ethic more concerned with
the process of decision making than with any absolute form of
decision.

Variously called the "new morality," "contextual ethics," "situation ethics," and in German *Gesinnungs-ethik* (attitudinal ethics),
this qualified ethical relativism has seemed to increasing numbers the
only viable moral expression for Christian faith in our time. This
does not mean that the "new" morality is really new, nor that it is
relevant only to the moral dilemma of twentieth-century man. But
the "new" morality is new in a relative sense; it is challenging old
and traditional theories of decision making. And it is peculiarly rele-

vant to contemporary man, for whom the relativity of things previously assumed to be unchanging is more and more obvious. Nonetheless, those who hold this attitude believe it is grounded in Scripture and represents a true expression of a Christian style for all ages.

"OLD" AND "NEW" MORALITIES

Although the terms "old" and "new" can be misleading, they help label opposing styles of decision making which are clashing head-on in our time. Consequently, it is instructive to examine the characteristics of the so-called "old" morality against which there is now a reaction.

The first thing which one must say about the "old" morality is that it is not simply synonymous with the Ten Commandments or the letter of the law. This equation is both misleading and unfair. The old morality, like the new morality, is not simply law and rules. It is instead an attitude toward law and rules and the way in which most responsibly to use them. It is an ethical attitude, an attitude about decision making. What then are the earmarks of this ethical attitude?

First, the old morality is primarily concerned with the letter or the content of the law. The old morality presupposes some set of rules, usually delivered as part of a religious tradition. This code defines appropriate forms for behavior and is binding in a way which covers all situations, cutting across the relativities of time and space. "Always" and "never" are key words in the vocabulary of the old moralist. One must always tell the truth, one must never have sexual intercourse outside of marriage, etc. Bishop Robinson puts it succinctly when he writes:

> The "old morality". . . locates the unchanging element in Christian ethics in the *content* of the commands. There are certain things which are always right, and others which are always wrong. These absolute Christian standards are eternally valid, and remain unchanging in the midst of relativity and flux. And it is this body of moral teaching, grounded firmly on the laws of God and the commands of Christ, which the Church exists to proclaim to every succeeding generation of men and women, whether they hear or whether they forbear.[3]

Such concern for the content of rules leads to a corresponding lack of concern for the context in which one applies the rules. From an old morality point of view, the context in which one decides whether or not to tell the truth makes little difference since the form of behavior has been prescribed *regardless of its context*. Where the old morality has recognized that situations differ, that context may influence consequences, that what is good for the goose may not be good for the gander, it has produced casuistry. Casuistry attempts to describe in advance certain conditions which may alter the context of a decision. Then it prescribes a new decision on the basis of altered conditions. Casuistic statements always begin "If" such and such a condition obtains, "then" this is what you should do. Although it has been traditionally suspect in Protestant circles, casuistry has long characterized Roman Catholic moral theology and Jewish thought. Indeed, a classic expression of casuistry is the covenant code in the Book of Deuteronomy.[4] And all of us tend to function, even if unconsciously, as primitive casuists. We anticipate certain circumstances and say: If such and such were the circumstance, then this is what I would do.

However, casuistry is still old morality. It still has a clear prescription for the form of behavior. And the primary concern of the casuist remains loyalty to that content. With the emergence of casuistry the old morality has simply refined its rules to come to grips with the ambiguities of human existence.

A second earmark of the old morality is its concern with externals. The law is external to the deciding individual. It exists independent of his value judgments and does not need to be appropriated as "his" law for its prescriptions to define what is good for him. The old morality is concerned with what psychologist Carl Rogers calls "an external locus of evaluation."[5] The point at which the "good" is determined is outside the individual. This external locus of evaluation is usually found in religious and cultural traditions which have been elevated to absolute status. However, it may be that the real source of the external loci to which the old morality appeals is a thoroughly "secular" cultural tradition, and that religion is only "used" (as Freud suggests[6]) to elevate culturally relative moral traditions to an absolute status. If it is the experience of a society, for example, that it is socially debilitating (i.e., threatening to the continued existence of the social unit) for young boys to sleep with their mothers, then best say that God says: You shall not sleep with your mother!

Because the old morality is primarily concerned with an external locus of evaluation, the "internal" dimensions of morality and decision making receive correspondingly less attention. Questions of motivation and ends usually occupy a secondary place in the thinking of old moralists. The reason why one makes a particular decision is not as important as the form of the decision and resulting behavior itself. The old morality makes little allowance for the insight that

> Of all things the greatest treason
> Is to do the right thing for the wrong reason.

Likewise, the old morality tends to draw a sharp distinction between ends and means (the rationale and the form of behavior) and to maintain that ends do not justify means.

A third earmark of the old morality is its emphasis on responsibility. The old morality is concerned with the responsibility of the individual moral agent. And when the old moralists speak of responsibility, they usually mean responsibility to fit behavior to the rules laid down by society or the religious establishment. Therefore, individual responsibility, according to old morality thinking, is responsibility *to the law*. The ultimate responsibility of the individual agent is to the moral code itself. Of course, this is often understood as responsibility to God or society or whoever gave the code. But in the actual process of making a decision, one's final loyalty is to the code itself.

This emphasis on responsibility to the law has two important by-products. First, it tends to make the moral code an object of faith. If one's final loyalty is to a particular code, then no other reality, cause, force, or spirit can intervene. This makes the law more important than God. In effect, it makes the law itself into a god. It is a form of idolatry which we might call "nomolatry." It is practiced by the individual who says, "under no circumstances" will I lie (rob, cheat, kill, commit tabooed sexual acts, etc.).

A second by-product of responsibility to the law is a corresponding de-emphasis of *freedom*. Old moralists do value freedom, but their concept of freedom is circumscribed by the law. This is the freedom to be good or bad, the traditional freedom to sin. But it is not the freedom to determine what is right and what is wrong. It is not the freedom to break the law and be justified in doing so.

A fourth important earmark of the old morality is its secularism. The old morality, as an ethical attitude, is not inherently related to a Christian style of life. This may surprise some critics of the old morality and shock some of its advocates. The old morality has for so long paraded itself in religious plumage (hence, the validity of Freud's indictment of religion [7]) that it has become identified with faith, especially where faith and religion are themselves confused. Indeed, the current debate between old and new moralities is still often portrayed as one between the defenders of religion and those who are antireligious. [8] (There is an element of truth in this insofar as new moralists stress the priority of faith over religiosity. But the portrayal gives the mistaken impression that the old morality is essentially religious *and* faith-oriented.) Actually, one can be a very good old moralist without any single ultimate commitment or faith, beyond a commitment to the law. And this is usually pluralistic in a way that makes the commitment polytheistic.

Let us compare the new morality with this traditional moral attitude.

In regard to the old morality's concern with the content of the law, the new morality is primarily concerned with its spirit or rationale. New moralists approach any code of rules with respect, but with the presupposition that all rules are finite and conditioned. They are always relative to the historical and cultural context which produces them. Likewise, the new morality assumes that enduring rules represent originally an attempt to apply some overarching principle in a way which yields workable guidelines for human behavior. The new morality holds that moral codes evolve in an historical process which is characterized by the application and interpretation of ultimate values in particular situations. They are not delivered full-blown by a supreme lawgiver, or by any supreme human council. The history of secular law appears to support this evolutionary view of moral codes.

The new morality attitude toward the letter of the law is one of respect but not adoration. The law as received (whether secular or religious) represents the collected wisdom of the culture. It therefore incorporates reasonable guidelines for behavior, to which one should pay heed, but by which one is not necessarily bound. One reason for the new moralist's respect for the letter is that he reads the spirit of the law off its letter. (Christians who identify Christianity with the spirit of the law over against a Judaism which is legalistic and committed to the letter should not forget this important point. Christianity presupposes the letter of the law as much as does Judaism. And the type of Jewish legalism and pharisaism depicted in the New Testament is not normative for all Judaism.) It is from a careful reading of a given set of commandments that the new moralist detects the rationale behind them. And it is this spirit which is ultimate. This spirit commands a loyalty higher than the letter of the law. In ethics which are self-consciously grounded in a theology, this is the God/spirit. And where God is understood as Love, as "He" is in the New Testament, the equation of the God/spirit with the ultimate rationale for decision making becomes clear. Because the spirit is given form and revealed in the letter of the law, new moralists should be clear that the law is essential, but not absolute. It is, as St. Paul says, a "schoolmaster to lead us to Christ." [9] Its function is to reveal, not to control. It is no more Christ himself for Paul than Christ is God.

Consequently, when a new moralist approaches a moral code, he comes with the question "Why?" He is concerned with rationales. When the old morality says: Thou shalt not kill, the new morality asks: Why? When the old morality says: Thou shalt not commit adultery, the new morality asks: Why? When the old morality says: Thou shalt not steal, the new morality asks: Why?, etc. And when the new morality detects a consistent rationale behind a given code (as it does with the Ten Commandments), then it affirms that this spirit takes primacy over the letter. And in those situations in which the spirit and the letter of the law are perceived to be in conflict, then the new morality holds that *faithful* decisions are those which conform to the spirit. This means that the form of behavior is left up to the individual as he perceives the demands of the spirit in a given situation. The process of decision making, however, is assumed to be constant: one is confronted with a decision; one asks what, all known and foreseeable factors considered, his ultimate commitment calls for; one decides and acts.

This emphasis on the primacy of the spirit points up the relationship between the new morality and a spirit-centered theology. Indeed, the new morality is a spirit-centered morality. It is inextricable from a theology where God is understood as spirit.[10] It is the only possible ethical expression of such a theology.

A second earmark of the new morality is its concern with internals rather than externals. In the dynamics of decision making, the new morality is primarily concerned with what Rogers calls an internal locus of evaluation. That is, the value which governs decisions is located within the perceptual process (the subjectivity) of the individual. This is similar to what Paul means by the distinction between what is written on cold tablets of stone and what is written "in the warm fleshiness of our hearts." [11] It is also similar to the call for an internalizing of the law in Deut. 6:6–9. What is most important in faithful decision making is what one believes to be ultimately important. And this is dependent on his faith (whether or not it is couched in religious terms) and his perception of the situation. The moral task is always to apply one's ultimate value to the circumstances, to ask what is most consistent with that value, and then to act. The final question for the new moralist is not "What do the rules say to do?" although he may ask this question in the process of reaching a responsible decision. The final question is "What do I believe, in terms of my deepest commitments, I ought to do?" Where that question is asked in a theological context, and where God is understood as Love, the question becomes simply: "What does Love command in this situation?" Or, to give Love explicit content, "What does the love of Christ (of the Cross) command in this situation?"

These are questions which emphasize an internal rather than an external locus of evaluation. They also express an internal process of decision making which is something more than mere conformity to external codes. They indicate what sociologist David Riesman calls an "inner-directed," as opposed to an "outer-directed" person.[12] And Riesman attributes greater stability to societies which produce inner-directed persons, just as Rogers attributes greater health to individuals with an internal locus of evaluation.

Third, where the old morality emphasizes responsibility to the law, the new morality emphasizes the freedom of the individual and his responsibility to a value which transcends the law. This freedom is not circumscribed by the law. In the New Testament it is rightly understood as freedom from the law.[13] This is not freedom to disregard the law. It is rather the freedom to break the law and still be morally right. It is freedom from the law as the ultimate determinant of right and wrong. It is freedom from the law as usurping the place of God. Such freedom presupposes commitment to a value which is greater than the law. This is what Tillich means by his emphasis on theonomy as reconciling the tension between heteronomy and autonomy.[14] Theonomous ethics, which are consistent with the new morality, assume that God is law, which is different from saying that a particular law is God. This is distinguished from heteronomy where the law comes from outside the individual (as with the old morality) and autonomy where the individual is a law unto himself (as with license). Without commitment, one would have no basis on which to question the letter of the law. One is not free to tear down idols except in the name of a higher God, a greater good. And new moralists who polemicize against the idolatry of the old morality should keep this firmly in mind.

The question of the relationship of freedom and responsibility is thoroughly paradoxical. When the old morality preaches responsibility to the rules, the new morality does not respond with an attack on responsibility *per se*. It instead affirms a higher responsibility, while reminding us that moral responsibility presupposes freedom. If you make a decision which conforms to the letter of the law, for example, your decision will only be responsible insofar as you were free in making it. To say that a decision is responsible simply because it conforms to a given code—when bribery, coercion, threat, or any number of morally questionable factors may be the rationale behind the decision—is to make irresponsibility into responsibility and to talk ethical nonsense. Responsible decisions are free decisions. And freedom becomes less than freedom when it is constricted by codes superimposed on an individual or a situation.

At the same time, this freedom is limited in two important ways. Herein lies the paradoxical nature of freedom. Moral freedom is limited first by the context in which decisions are made, which usually offers only certain alternatives and not others. For example, I am free at this moment to remain at my typewriter, to take a nap, to go swimming, to go fishing, etc. But I am not free to go for a drive since my wife has the car. In a less contingent realm, I am free to involve myself in the civil rights struggle in a way sympathetic to black (really human) rights. But I am not free to become a black man, even though in the current temper of this struggle that appears an attractive option.

Second, moral freedom is also limited by one's ultimate commitments. This is a point which is often missed by those who confuse
freedom with license. (And they may be found in the ranks of both
the critics and the advocates of the new morality.) *Real freedom is
found only in obedience.*[15] This is not obedience to any pluralistic
set of rules. It is obedience to a single ultimate value, one's ideal,
one's God. True morality consists of the free and responsible application of that value in a particular context. Any alternative form of
freedom is either unfreedom or license. And license, properly understood, is unfreedom because it binds you to a plurality of values.
Without care and discrimination you do what you please in any
situation. The bondage of license, like bondage to the law, is arbitrary and inconsistent with itself. It does not take the circumstances
of situations seriously. But just as there is only a thin line between
license and legalism, so also there is only a thin line between license
and moral freedom. St. Augustine said: "Love with care and do as
you please." [16] That is a new morality statement. It presupposes the
commitment implied in the phrase "love with care." It is something
quite different from simply doing what you please. It is instead doing what you *will* in obedience to the God of Love. One of the regular
morning collects in the Episcopal *Book of Common Praye*r describes
the deity with the phrase "whose service is perfect freedom." That is
the mandate for the new morality. It articulates the paradox of freedom in obedience.

Finally, the "faithful" dimension of the new morality must be juxtaposed to the secularism of the old morality. This is closely related
to freedom in obedience. The new morality is a committed morality.
The primacy of the spirit over the letter of the law presupposes commitment to the spirit. The new morality is then a morality of faith.
This does not, however, mean that one can only be a new moralist
if he holds his faith commitment in a particular form. It does not
even mean that his faith commitment must be perceived in religious
terms. To say that the new morality is a faith morality means only
that it presupposes a faith, whatever form it may take. It presupposes
response to a supreme value which one attempts to apply in every
situation. This is why the identification of the new morality with the
forces of anti-faith can only be made by those who fail to make a
meaningful distinction between faith as a style of life and religion as

certain supernatural beliefs. Such thinking characterizes advocates as well as opponents of the new morality.

Some who applaud this kind of moral thinking persist in separating it from the commitment in which it is grounded. The new morality cannot tolerate such a divorce because its basis for decision making is undercut. What was called a new morality then becomes a new license. At this point, critics of the new morality are justified in using their "antinomian" and "licentious" epithets, although they are criticizing a straw man. It is not the new morality as it has been set forth here and by other responsible spokesmen.[17]

RELIGIOUS IDEALISM

This new morality involves a radical religious idealism. Idealism means commitment to an ideal and the attempt to apply one's ideal in real situations. It should not be juxtaposed to realism, so that "idealistic" people and ideas are rejected as "unrealistic." On the contrary, the new morality is understood by its proponents as an eminently realistic and realizable ethical attitude.

This idealism is radical because of its ultimate and uncompromising nature. It is not a "moderate" idealism which applies the ideal in some situations but not in others. Such unwillingness to invoke the law of love in *every* situation puts the lie to idealism and turns the new morality into the same kind of moral hypocrisy which has often characterized the old morality.[18] At the same time, this idealism may also be called "religious" insofar as it is grounded in some kind of ultimate commitment. It has about it the character of religious zeal.

It is important to stress the idealistic nature of the new morality because it is often criticized as either unrealistic or incapable of fulfillment. Critics posit the impossibility of living by an ideal and cite the need for greater controls on human behavior than the new morality is willing to impose. This criticism often comes from those who hold a negative view of human nature, and who consequently fear the moral freedom which the new morality advocates. Such critics say that the new morality is for saints, not sinners. Or they suggest that the new morality presupposes greater moral sophistication and commitment than most people have.

There is an element of truth in these charges. It is, for example, true that it is virtually impossible to live consistently by a single ideal and to apply that ideal in every decision. No one knows this better than those who try to live by a situational ethic. Human self-centeredness often confuses the issue, distorts the way in which one sees a particular situation, and usurps the primacy of one's ultimate ideal. But the record of the old law-centered morality on controlling self-centeredness is not very impressive. Indeed, the old morality would appear to provide more camouflage under which to mask one's sin as righteousness and a greater potential for self-deception.

In this regard, the new morality is also a penitent morality. By virtue of his idealism one is called to an awareness of the extent to which he constantly falls short of his ideal. It is therefore appropriate for him to confess these shortcomings (whether formally or informally) in terms of specific situations in which he has failed to live by the law of love. Where one's morality is situational, so is one's penitence. This type of penitence is characteristic of the Christian tradition. However, although old moralists confess sins, traditional Christian penitence is not consistent with their ethical attitude. As soon as one compromises moral idealism with a code-centered morality, it becomes possible to act in a fully righteous way. As soon as righteousness is defined by a universal code, it becomes universally achievable. It is, after all, possible to keep the rules. Hence, the self-righteousness of the Pharisee in the New Testament parable.[19] A moral attitude which is anything less than fully idealistic is also potentially self-righteous.

The new morality also affirms an optimistic understanding of human nature. This is the other side of a paradoxical doctrine of man which takes sin seriously. Although the new moralist experiences himself as constantly falling short of his ideal, he also believes himself capable of fulfilling it in a given moment. He approaches every decision with the assumption that it is possible for him to act in a selfless and loving way. Otherwise, why ask the question: What does love demand in this situation? The new morality takes seriously the New Testament affirmation that because Jesus is the Son of God men of faith have been given the power to become sons of God.[20] That is, because the ideal is revealed as realizable in the man Jesus, it is revealable and realizable in each of us. This does not contradict the "realistic" understanding that we often fail to realize our ideal. It is simply the other side of the coin. It is thoroughly biblical, in spite of religious attempts to undercut the Bible's high estimate of human moral potential. Hence, there is a half-truth in the charge that the new morality is for saints, not sinners. But one need not juxtapose those terms. After all, the Church has traditionally understood itself to be both a community of sinners and the communion of saints.[21]

The moral freedom of this new morality is also dangerous, as critics suggest. It is very dangerous to allow an individual to determine what is right and wrong in a given situation according to his own highest ideal. Ironically, it is much more dangerous than most old moralists realize. This is because the measure of danger within the old morality is the law. When an old moralist says that freedom is dangerous, he has in mind the breaking of the law. When a new moralist says that freedom is dangerous, he has in mind doing something which is unloving. That is a real danger, but it is one against which the old morality with all its rules has never been able to develop an adequate safeguard. It also represents the price the new moralist pays for his moral freedom. You cannot, after all, force a person to act in a loving way. You can, however, call upon him to act this way. The new morality is dangerous because it couches its call in terms which presuppose his capacity to love. The old morality mistakenly assumes that it has avoided this danger because it does not make this presupposition so clear.

Finally, the new morality presupposes a high degree of moral sophistication and commitment. The dimension of commitment has already been discussed. The dimension of "sophistication" needs to be addressed since it is often assumed that a contextual ethic is "all right for grown-ups, but not for children" (or college students!). Such an assumption supposes that moral sophistication is a function of social, intellectual, and physiological maturity. This is not necessarily the case. It is as possible for a small child to learn the ethical attitude of the new morality as it is for an adult. The moral sophistication presupposed has to do with the capacity to distinguish meaningfully between rules and their rationales. And many children can do this more effectively than adults. Their capacity to do so depends, among other things, on the ways in which rules are presented and punishments are administered and explained. Ethical attitudes, like other attitudes, are learned. The new morality, consequently, has serious implications for moral education.[22] Of course, the religious idealism of the new morality need not be couched in religious terms to be idealistic. One can be a thoroughly "secular" new moralist, as some who call themselves ethical humanists are. The ethical culture movement in America has often provided a communal home for those who reject the religious basis of ethics but maintain a healthy moral/ religious idealism. This movement, significantly, was founded by a renegade rabbi, Felix Adler. To this day, ethical culture continues to draw a large proportion of its constituency from members of the Jewish community who subscribe to the ethics but not the theological assumptions of classical Judaism.

THE PLACE OF SIN

The idealistic dimension of the new morality implies a particular understanding of sin. One cannot discuss the human capacity to love without also positing the human capacity for unlove, at least as long as one takes seriously moral freedom and responsibility. Within a new morality understanding, where God is love, sin is unlove.

The problem with speaking of sin today is that persistent misuse has practically destroyed the theological usefulness of the word. To define sin by the law and to equate sin with breaking the law dethrones the word from the high place it once held in the theologian's vocabulary and still holds in the biblical vocabulary. Where the form of sin is defined by a code, men develop a catalog of sins (as the Roman Catholic Church has traditionally done, e.g., in the distinction between "mortal" and "venial" sins, and the categorical listing of each) and the word comes to refer to particular acts which break the rules. Therefore, one speaks of his sins and means specific "bad" things he has done, where badness is defined by a preconceived set of rules.

In the Bible, however, sin is much more than this. In the Bible, sin is a characteristic of human nature which is particularly evident in the decision-making process. In the Garden of Eden myth,[23] for example, sin is the choice of man against the situational command of the God/spirit and in favor of his own self-interest. Likewise, in the New Testament, the Greek word for sin (*'amartia*) means "missing the mark," i.e., not being fully loving in one's decisions and behavior. Sin then becomes the opposite of love. Sin is unlove. Therefore, only those acts are sinful which are unloving, where love is defined by the figure of Jesus. Here, a doctrine of sin is the logical corollary of a doctrine of love. But there can be no contingent definition of sin beyond that involved in identifying a particular medium for the God/spirit. No single act is always sinful because there might be a situation in which that act would be the most loving response.

Sin is then more appropriately viewed as a state of being than as a specific act,[24] although sin is only revealed through specific acts. Likewise, it is more appropriate to speak of one's *sin* than one's *sins,* although the individual has the responsibility to identify his own sinful acts. This process, as we have seen, is fundamental to a Christian understanding of penitence and confession.

One important distinction between old and new moralities is that they assume different norms for their understandings of righteousness. Another important distinction is that the old morality tends to derive its ethics from the "sin" end of the sin/love polarity while the new morality tends to derive its ethics from the "love" end. The old moralist examines a particular decision and asks: What are the sinful possibilities which must be controlled or eliminated in this type of decision? And then he develops a rule which always covers decisions regarding this form of behavior, regardless of their context. Such ethics are derived primarily from a doctrine of sin. The new moralist, on the other hand, examines a particular decision in context and asks: What does love demand in this situation? The primary question is not "What are the dangers?" but rather "What are the possibilities?" These ethics are derived from a doctrine of love. Such a doctrine does not ignore sin. It simply sees sin in a different perspective.

Much of the debate between old and new moralists hinges, then, on different theoretical starting points for judgments of right and wrong. They emphasize differing aspects of the biblical doctrine of man. Insofar as both old and new moralities are argued on biblical grounds, this represents at once their commonality and their contrast as ethical attitudes. This cannot be ignored if the current debate is not to degenerate into simply trading epithets like "antinomian," "legalist," etc.

SOME APPLICATIONS

The new morality does not evoke very much emotional ferment as long as it remains theoretical.[25] It is usually considered either harmless or idiosyncratic until implications for concrete situations are spelled out. A concerned mother writes: "I agree that my daughter should make her own decisions, but not when it means ruining her life!" Of course, what is "ruining" one's life is also a relative judgment, contingent on context. A young man agonizes over whether or not to violate selective service laws as an act of conscience. He knows that one decision may mean several years of his life in jail. The alternative may be participation in a war he considers fundamentally immoral. Suddenly, the new morality is more than simply theoretical. It sharpens the tension between moral idealism and utilitarianism, although it does not make them irreconcilable—except situationally.

Before illustrating situational ethics, therefore, an important caveat: *It is impossible to say what the new morality says you ought to do in a particular situation.* To try to codify situational thinking in any universal way is to reduce the new morality to casuistry. (Joseph Fletcher calls the new morality a "neo-casuistry" [26] but he is careful to note that this is a flexible casuistry and not the kind of codified casuistry which is usually identified with the old morality. Although, within his careful definitions, he is correct, I prefer not to use the word "casuistry" in regard to the new morality.) What to do in a particular situation can only be determined by the individual who stands in that situation and is aware of the many nuances which make it unique.

Unfortunately, well-intentioned interpreters have often attempted to spell out the new morality in ways that make it simply a more liberal version of the code to which the old morality has always made its appeal. I do not intend to do this. One cannot prescribe *in abstracto* the conditions under which, for example, premarital intercourse or civil disobedience might be morally commendable. In such a discussion one can only give illustrations in which it is impossible to cite all the circumstances of a given situation. However, the new moralist can say unequivocally that there are situations in which premarital intercourse or civil disobedience might be morally commendable. On the other hand, he will respond with some impatience to those who persist in asking: What is the right thing for me to do in this situation? To them, he may justifiably put another question: Who made me a judge over you? [27]

Four broad areas of decision making in which contemporary students experience the most intense moral dilemmas are:

1. *Sex*—The ethics of sexuality is a traditional focal point for any systematic morality.[28] If Freud is right, problems of a sexual nature are at the root of all moral prescriptions.[29] And the research for a responsible mode of sexual self-expression is at the forefront of most ethical systems. Sex is also a prominent dimension of the contemporary moral dilemma—so much so that in some circles the word *morality* has become synonymous with sexual morality.

On the modern American scene, the prominence of sex as a domain of decision making is aggravated by a cultural heritage which includes attitudes toward sexuality that are both negative and unrealistic. It is not within the scope of this book to elaborate these attitudes or to demonstrate their debilitating effect on sexual morality.[30] At the same time, these attitudes influence the context in which an individual today makes sexual decisions. Consequently, they cannot be ignored by a stituationist. Briefly, they are the attitudes that (1) sexuality itself, including the parts of the body identified with sexual differentiation, is bad and dangerous, or at least slightly tainted; and (2) there is a radical discontinuity between the human spirit and the human body which makes the latter a moral encumbrance to the former. The body is bad and its appetites cause people to make morally bad decisions.

Both of these attitudes have deeply influenced sexual mores in twentieth-century America. They are both also unbiblical and inconsistent with the insights of modern psychology.[31] The concern of the new moralist, however, is not so much with the invalidity of these attitudes and the assumptions which underlie them. That is an issue he will have to decide on other than moral grounds. His concern is rather with these attitudes as they inform the context in which he makes his decisions and the extent to which they are "part of him."

Consequently, when confronted with a decision regarding a sexual act, a situationist asks himself some pointed questions about the meaning of his act and of his sexuality. These are questions which the old morality rarely asks, since the old morality has essentially only one question for heterosexual relations: Are you married to each other? And behind that question is a clear rule which says: If you're married, yes. If you're not married, no. But the new moralist is not satisfied with such answers because his final court of appeal is higher than the rules. He has a criterion (love) by which he knows that there are situations and occasions in which it is immoral to engage in sexual relations in marriage and moral to engage in them outside of marriage.

How then is he to decide in *this* situation, whether or not married? Among other things, by asking questions about the meaning of the sexual act and of sexuality itself. How do I view my sexuality? Is it something good, which is essentially part of me and my identity? If so, any act of sexual expression is an expression of me, my total selfhood. This is more than simply my genital needs, what might be called my genitality as over against my whole sexuality. Or, is my sexuality something bad and tainted, not integral to the real me? Is it an attachment which must be concealed and only used to fulfill earthy, bodily needs? If so, an act of sexual self-expression may be an act of detachment, having no more moral dimensions than a game of tennis. According to such a view, the act itself is personal only insofar as the body of another person is required. (This is contrary to the first option, where, if *my* selfhood and identity is involved, so is that of my partner.) Or is my sexuality essentially something neutral? Is it detached from me and the person I am and only good or bad depending on how I use it? If so, moral considerations will only enter into my decision making insofar as my "use" of my sexuality might hurt someone else. Whether or not the act itself expresses love for the sexual partner will be a lesser consideration.

All of these attitudes toward sexuality are common in our time. Some such attitude informs the context in which every decision regarding sexual behavior is made. To ignore such attitudes in oneself (as the old morality tends to do) is to make immorality into morality. It is to say, for example, that a demanding husband's rape of his wife is morally more commendable than premarital intercourse between consenting adults. Such a moral judgment might be consistent with a codified morality. But it would be highly questionable according to a morality which appeals to the law of love as defined by Jesus of Nazareth.

Beyond the attitudes cited, the new moralist also asks questions about foreseeable consequences of sexual relations. Here the old morality has tried to have its cake and eat it too. Traditionally, old moralists have said without condition: heterosexual relations before marriage are inherently evil. And then they have supported this with a situational argument: such relations might result in a pregnancy with an unwanted child and other related social complications. The result of this doublethink within the Churches is that with the advent of reasonably foolproof methods of conception control, young people have understandably reasoned that since the key consequence has been altered, the key variable controlled, an act once universally unacceptable is now universally acceptable. The moral shallowness of much contemporary thinking in this area is the price we are paying for the Church's moral shallowness in brandishing the threat of pregnancy as *the* deterrent to premarital intercourse. The same could be said of any of the relativistic threats currently bandied about by some preachers, e.g., loss of virginity and its effect on marital happiness, habitual promiscuity, venereal disease, etc.

When the new moralist asks his question about consequences, he is aware that this is but one dimension of the context in which his decision must be made. He is also aware that consequences are usually many-faceted, and that no one consequence represents the only consideration in reaching a responsible decision. In sexual relations, he will also be concerned with his and his partner's attitude toward a potential child. He should be concerned with their readiness for the responsibilities of parenthood, emotionally and economically. And he will likewise be concerned with the consequences of the sexual act for other people and other relationships, e.g., parents, other lovers, etc.

There are, of course, other dimensions of the context in which every sexual decision is made. But, in every decision regarding a sexual act, the final responsibility of the individual is to ask not: What do the rules say? but rather: Everything of which I am aware considered, what course of action is most consistent with my ultimate ideal? Where that ideal is concern for the other, the considerations will include concern for a number of others in addition to one's sexual partner. And this kind of moral thinking holds for all forms of sexual self-expression, masturbation and homosexuality included. According to this thinking, no form of sexual self-expression is inherently evil. To the repeated question: Is it right for me to do this or that in my sex life? the new moralist will continue to answer: That all depends. . . . And one of the things it depends on is you—who you are and what your frame of reference is, as well as the foreseeable consequences of your behavior. More than that, no morality which refuses to make your decisions for you can say.[32]

2. *Civil disobedience*—Recent political developments have focused attention on the moral issue of civil disobedience. Civil disobedience is systematic violation of the civil law in an effort to change it. When it is true civil disobedience, this lawbreaking assumes that the law broken is unjust and not amenable to alteration in any other way. Illustrative of such a situation in recent times were the voting regulations in certain states whereby the black man was effectively deprived of his franchise. But by virtue of this deprivation the black man has also been powerless to change the law through the usual constitutional means.

Civil disobedience in such a context appeals to a principle or "law" higher than the civil law itself. Usually this principle is an abstraction such as "justice," "equality," "neighbor-love," which is not itself spelled out in any new code. When civil disobedience is undertaken on explicitly religious grounds, the higher value takes the form of a religious tradition. Consequently, civil disobedience can be an expression of new morality thinking and decision making. In the name of a higher ideal one violates the prescribed rules in an effort, among other things, to bring those rules into greater conformity with the higher ideal. Where the ideal is identified with the spirit of the law itself, then a particular law is attacked as not only unjust, but also illegal or "unconstitutional." In the same way the new morality attacks rigid adherence to certain biblical precepts as itself unbiblical, i.e., contrary to the spirit of the biblical law.

In spite of its relatively recent resuscitation, civil disobedience is a very old phenomenon. It was allegedly practiced by Abraham, David, Socrates, Jesus, Luther, and Gandhi. Martin Luther King, in justifying his own civil disobedience,[33] leaned heavily on the writings of Paul, Augustine, and Luther. The story of Abraham and Isaac represents a model case. As Kierkegaard rightly points out,[34] judged by the law, Abraham's intended sacrifice of Isaac is murder. But Abraham transcends the law in obedience to his God. That is the whole point of the myth. Abraham's reluctant willingness to slaughter his own son is an instance of what Kierkegaard calls "the teleological suspension of the ethical." Ordinary ethical considerations are suspended in the pursuit of a higher ultimate goal, obedience to one's God. Likewise, in an instance commended by Jesus, David enters the Temple and has his hungry soldiers eat the consecrated bread [35]— an act of disobedience, for a Jew, but done in the name of a higher principle. Socrates systematically teaches in violation of the law of his time in order to demonstrate the injustice of that law, finally by his imprisonment and his death.[36] Jesus picks grain on the sabbath in order to fulfill human need. Luther defied the constituted civil and ecclesiastical authority of his time in the name of truthfulness to his God. And for almost half a century, Gandhi waged an incredible campaign of nonviolent noncooperation (civil disobedience) against the injustice which the white man had inflicted on the black man in South Africa and India. Americans who see patriotism affronted by civil disobedience in the current civil rights and peace movements should remember that the celebrated Boston tea party was in its time seen as an act of sheer vandalism!

To recognize moral integrity in civil disobedience is not to ignore that it can cloak "uncivil" disobedience. It is not uncommon for uncivil disobedience (anarchy, lawlessness, license) to parade itself under the banner of civil disobedience. However, there are certain criteria which can at least help the individual make discriminating judgments about the civility of his own disobedience.

First, because civil disobedience appeals to a higher principle, the means of disobedience should be consistent with that principle. This is the obedient dimension of the freedom which civil disobedience expresses. If the higher value is concern for the neighbor, for example, even when he is one's enemy, the means of civil disobedience will generally be nonviolent. It is usually not in the interest of one's fellow man to inflict bodily harm on him, even in the pursuit of his welfare. The student protester who slugs a policeman has probably compromised the idealistic basis of his disobedience. Of course, this is not true where his ideology is revolutionary (calling for an overthrow of established structures regardless of means), but revolution is no longer *civil* disobedience.

This is why so much civil disobedience has been carefully disciplined and meticulously nonviolent. This has been particularly true of movements headed by Gandhi and King, each of whom appealed to self-conscious religious values. This is not true of uncivil disobedience which often acts in ways blatantly inconsistent with its stated goal. For example, the action of a mob which burns and destroys government property in protest against an unjust regime is probably uncivil disobedience. Among other things, it appears to lack the necessary ingredient of discipline. The paradoxical dimension of obedience in all civil disobedience is missing.

However, there is no immutable, universal canon defining what constitutes "good" and "bad" civil disobedience. That would codify civil disobedience and make it contrary to the new morality. For example, although civil disobedience in my experience has always been nonviolent, that reflects a particular commitment. Nonviolence can no more be established as a universal than can any other criterion for civil disobedience. But one can still distinguish civil disobedience from its uncivil counterpart—among other things, by the consistency of its means with its stated goal and ultimate ideal. This is why it is fallacious for the new moralist to make any final distinction between ends and means, since the two always inform one another. (Fletcher says flatly that according to the new morality the end does justify the means. But this is an oversimplification, since the principle that the end justifies the means can itself become a law. Historically this has had dire consequences. To make any clear dichotomy between ends and means is to miss the subtlety of the new morality insight that the two are inextricable. Fletcher seems to recognize this.[37])

Second, civil disobedience should be marked by concern for the integrity of the legal system it violates. Civil disobedience is not anti-law but super-law. Its appeal is not so much against the law as it is above the law. Its goal is not to destroy the law, but to purify it (as well as to satisfy the demands of conscience over those of the law). It is concerned with the maintenance of what is usually called "law and order," even at the price of a temporary rupture in that state. Consequently, civil disobedience demonstrates respect for the law in the very act of breaking it. This is usually accomplished by "disobeying" openly and by not resisting arrest or subverting the processes of normal law enforcement. By such means, civil disobedience puts the lie to those who call it lawless and demonstrates its support for law in principle. Like the new morality of which it is an expression, civil disobedience should never be understood as a call for the abolition of law itself. Thus, Socrates does not resist arrest. And he declines the offer of escape from jail because it would undo his witness against the injustice of the law, and his support of its spirit.[38] Likewise, the widespread nonresistance which characterized Gandhi's and King's movements demonstrates that they were intent on the reform, not the abolition, of the law. In response to those who considered Jesus lawless and the Sermon on the Mount an attack on the law itself, he responded: I have come not to destroy the law, but to fulfill it.[39]

This is not necessarily the case with uncivil disobedience, which can be both surreptitious and underhanded. Activities of the Ku Klux Klan, for example, which could appear as civil disobedience in devotion to a higher value, fail to demonstrate respect for the law by attempting to evade detection. Likewise, bribery and coercion of police and court officials would appear generally to be uncivil disobedience insofar as the due process of law is subverted.

Civil disobedience is then a classic expression of the ethical attitude called the new morality. But, like other expressions of this attitude, every act of civil disobedience is subject to the utmost discipline, care, discrimination, and *obedience*. Of course, according to the new morality, that should also be true of every act of civil obedience and conformity to the established order. Thus, the young man who submits to the draft in our present situation is as answerable, morally speaking, as he who refuses to submit. Every decision should be marked by discipline, care, discrimination, and ultimately by obedience. That is what makes the new morality a more difficult ethical attitude to practice than the old morality.

3. *Pacifism*—One of the growing moral movements of our time is the new peace movement. Particularly as it has focused on American foreign policy, involvement in southeast Asia, and the war in Vietnam, this movement has evoked widespread sympathy from the present generation of college students, as well as from other morally sensitive Americans. Indeed, as in the civil rights movement, students have provided a good deal of the raw manpower which has forced the peace movement on the public conscience. The underlying issues and values, traditionally identified with pacifism, are illustrative of both old and new morality types of thinking.

The classical and simplistic pacifist position has been an unswerving opposition to war, violence, and the taking of human life. "Thou shalt not kill" is taken as an absolute and universal moral law. On such grounds, those who identify themselves as pacifists have from time to time also been counted in the ranks of opposition to fertility control, mercy killing, capital punishment, and even among antivivisectionists. However *generally* consistent with the law of love a refusal to kill may be, such thinking is not compatible with the new morality. It is not consistent with "deciding for yourself," since the decision about killing is already made in advance for you.

To say that "Thou shalt not kill" is a moral imperative which cannot be adjusted to conditions is to revert to the old morality. It is to avoid the dangerous relativism of the new morality and opt instead for an apparently safer form of an old familiar bondage. In spite of the commendable opposition to the status quo which this position sometimes entails, and the courageous acts to which it has given rise, it represents a mode of decision making which the new moralist is unable to embrace.

Does the new moralist then endorse any war which justifies itself through appeal to political, economic, or social circumstances, as all wars do? No. Insofar as the new moralist finds the pacifist position generally compatible with his own love-ethic, he will usually also be a "situational pacifist." Situational pacifism does not mean simply that one will be a pacifist where the status quo favors his self-interest and a belligerent where it does not. That would only be true if the ultimate ideal of situational pacifism were self-interest, not self-giving love. The situational pacifist finds himself instead in the strange position of affirming most pacifist efforts to inhibit war making, while holding out the option of a *situation* in which he himself would take a human life in the name of neighbor-love.

What might such a situation be? Gandhi is reported to have been asked once what he would have done and whether he would have engaged in violence or the taking of life in the Warsaw ghetto under the Nazis. The picture painted there [40] is one of almost inhuman exploitation and subhuman living conditions. Gandhi's reply? He is alleged to have responded that there are some situations in which it may be necessary to take a life in the name of one's own humanity or the humanity of another. Presumably, "another" includes one's oppressor. This is a thoroughly situational answer. Yet Gandhi is known as a pacifist. And his apparent equivocality raises all of those agonizing questions with which a situational pacifist must live.

What, for example, are the criteria for gauging what is human and what is inhuman? Isn't this simply a new abstraction for the moral absolute, as subject to rationalization in one's self-interest as any abstraction—including Love? How does one preserve the humanity of his oppressor by killing him?

Dietrich Bonhoeffer (significantly a forerunner of modern situational thinking) reportedly endured similar agonies in reaching a decision to become involved in the abortive plot on Adolf Hitler's life. Here the ultimate Love principle was interpreted to call for complicity in an act of violence on the basis of the end justifying the means—situationally. Hitler's death (by any means!) was deemed important to bringing an end to the inhuman liquidation of the Jews, which he both headed and symbolized. Bonhoeffer's decision was thoroughly situational, by a man who was essentially nonviolent. It was not an easy decision, based on any "eye for an eye" legalism, and it probably eventually cost Bonhoeffer his own life. Its complexity is the complexity of situational pacifism. This is analogous to the complexity of situational monogamy, or situational law abiding, or any other general practice which the new moralist follows in a "most, but not all, cases" frame of reference.

Indeed, the new moralist whose frame of reference is explicitly Christian would seem to be forced to this kind of situational pacifism, particularly in the present context of international relations. The alternatives are simply impossible for him. He cannot embrace an absolute pacifism, however neat and attractive this posture may be in most cases. Its intrinsic legalism does not allow for morally significant differences in situations, and contradicts that style of decision making which calls finally for "deciding for yourself." At the same time, any kind of general justification for violence, the making of war, or the taking of human lives, is equally unacceptable. That too ignores the complexities of situations. And it provides a rationalization for behavior which appears generally inconsistent with the love-ethic of the Gospel.

One might suppose, for example, that a situational pacifist would subscribe to the classical doctrine of a just war. This is true in principle but not in fact. Insofar as the doctrine of a just war asserts that there may be occasions when in the name of love it is necessary to take the life of another, it expresses new morality thinking. But insofar as it attempts to define the conditions in advance (by offering, for example, such unlovely justifications for war as the preservation of a Christian society), it is unpalatable to the new morality. This is exactly what has happened historically to the doctrine of a just war. It has degenerated into a form of casuistry. Spelling out in advance the conditions under which one can kill is old morality thinking. Indeed, the preservation of a particular social code has often been invoked as justification under the doctrine of a just war. Thus, colonial wars were fought to impose a monogamous sexual ethic on the "heathen," to suppress cannibalism, or, in modern times, to halt communism, etc. Such casuistry, and the moral hypocrisy to which it can lead, are incompatible with the new morality. However, in principle the doctrine of justified killing is consistent with a situational ethic.

Interestingly, large numbers of those involved in the current peace agitation in the United States appear to be articulating a situational pacifism. One factor which makes the new peace movement "new," as compared with the peace movements of the thirties, is its thoroughgoing ethical relativism. This is marked by the emergence of conscientious objectors to selective service on the basis of a particular war. It is also reflected in increasing support for the peace movement from those whose consciences have been stirred only by the injustice of a particular military involvement.

4. *Revolt Against Institutionalized Authority*—Still another moral dimension of the lives of many young people is their revolt against institutionalized authority. This has been evident in the civil rights and peace movements, and in increased questioning of the morality of the Church and other traditional institutions, including academic institutions. This revolt is evidenced today in the mistrust with which many young people view any who are invested with institutional authority. It is dramatically portrayed in the 1964 Berkeley slogan that "you can't trust anyone over 30."

As this revolt presently stirs on our campuses in friction between students and college administrators, it appears that it will become larger in numbers, more pervasive in influence, and more dramatic in style, before it subsides. It is also becoming clear that this revolt has a moral basis. What is being revolted against is not authority itself but rather the immoral ways in which authority perpetuates itself and decisions regarding persons are made. The real crux of the present student unrest is a moral protest against the immorality (according to a Christian/humanist ideal) of making structures and systems more important than persons. The moral outrage of student unrest is perhaps best illustrated by the disdain and disaffection with which students speak of the "establishment" or the "system." Both of these amorphous nouns designate a whole syndrome of institutionalized decision making and the values which appear to govern it.

Many students today are invoking the spirit of the educational establishment against its form in a particular situation. Such a moral protest has clear affinities with the new morality. What many student protesters are saying to their educational institutions is: Live up to what you say you are. Live up to the principles embodied in your charter! Practice rather than simply preach free inquiry and free expression of ideas—as opposed to inquiry and expression in only those areas where public opinion will not be alienated. Practice rather than simply preach a real concern for effective classroom teaching— as opposed to a concern for publication and research and other more marketable products of the educational establishment. Practice rather than simply preach flexibility in matters of curriculum planning and grading. Practice as well as preach the kind of participatory democracy to which most respectable institutions claim to be committed. Practice rather than simply preach student responsibility for student social behavior. Practice rather than simply preach authentic openness to the self-expression of black people and to their meaningful involvement in the life of academia, as both students and teachers. This could involve our educational institutions in a healthy rethinking of their own rationale or spirit. This includes those qualifications or "standards" for appointment or admission which tend to be legalistically (not situationally!) adhered to. In the present cultural context, this often means a continuation of de facto racial discrimination by institutions and individuals who disavow such an intention.

Such an appeal to the spirit of free education over against its present posture in many institutions is thoroughly compatible with the new morality. And the sooner college administrators and trustees abandon their old morality ways of thinking about students ("They are incapable of assuming responsibility for their own lives"; "They simply want to make life easier for themselves"; "They are the pawns of subversive agitators or members of the faculty"; "They do not know what kind of education they need"; "They break the rules they already have," etc.) the sooner will they recognize that morality itself is an issue here; and the sooner will there be some hope of reconciliation where the chasm presently seems to be widening.

At the same time, students need to ask themselves whether the form of their protest is consistent with the high principles it espouses.

There is something tragicomic in the student who invokes ideals of human dignity while dehumanizing the college president in a way which removes from him all vestige of dignity, treats him as a symbol rather than a person. And there is irony in the student who laments the hypocrisy of college policies on drugs and sexual behavior, while doing nothing to change things beyond covertly breaking the rules. Likewise, there is moral doublethink in the black student movement when it purports to combat racist policies with transparently racist rhetoric or racially exclusive policies. And this is not made less ironic by appeal to racial cohesion and awareness as a goal, however commendable that may be *in the present situation.* Ends may still need to have some recognizable consistency with means.

As with the new peace movement, the new morality can give no *carte blanche* approval to the current revolt against institutionalized authority. When a new moralist, however, senses a kindred spirit in such a movement, he can and will link arms with those who protest in support of the morality of their cause. Only in this way is he in a position, among other things, to call such movements to task for their departures from their own high ideals. Only in this way can he fulfill the prophetic task. It too is a function of all biblical morality.

A PERSONAL NOTE

To advocate the kind of qualified moral relativism presented here has been, in my experience, to invite speculation about one's own morality. Any such attack on rules as absolutes tends to make one suspect of personal libertinism on the one hand and encouraging anarchy on the other. Consequently, two personal questions that I encounter most frequently as responses to this "new" morality are: (1) Do you make your own decisions in this way? Are you really this free? (2) Do you raise your children to be free in this way? If so, how? Are there no rules in your house?

By way of closing this chapter, I should like to address myself at a personal level to those two questions.

With regard to the first, it is probable that none of us is as free in his decision making as he would like to be, or would like to think he is. We are all responsible to a proliferation of social demands and expectations. These qualify and often compromise our decisions and what we like to see as our moral idealism. This is one reason that some Christians (including new moralists) find meaning in regular confession of sin. Still, within the limits of our faintheartedness, some measure of freedom from the law is a live option, at least in the author's experience.

I would like to think, therefore, that my decision making in a given instance is never predetermined by a set of rules or expectations. My behavior may however be predictable for those who know me and understand me. And that predictability does not always run in a nonconformist direction. If it did, I could easily become a slave to a new law—the law of nonconformity.

I also hope that my decision making is marked by responsiveness and sensitivity to the situations in which I find myself. Of course, this is not always the case. Pride, self-centeredness, and simple carelessness blunt the sensitivities of each of us at times. But, the law provides no built-in safeguards against human insensitivity. And on a continuum which runs from responding to the demands of rules to responding to the situation in terms of what (according to my ideal) is best, I would always prefer to err toward the later end.

All of this adds up to saying that the quality which I cherish in my personal decision making is *openness*. This means first of all openness to the situation itself—in all of its nuances, meanings, and the potential consequences of alternative decisions. But it also means openness to the demands of Love in the situation. It has been my experience that a preoccupation with the demands of the law can constrict this openness. But such openness is a risky business. It requires courage which is sometimes lacking. It can require doing what is unexpected, illegal, or socially tabooed. It may mean paying a penalty, either legally imposed or through incurring the disfavor of those who do not understand. In my experience, it has meant all of this, although only in trivial measure.

More than this, I do not know what one can honestly say about his own decision making. It is generally a complicated morass of guilt, fear, rationalized self-interest, habit, and moral idealism. But the fact that it is not always neat need not qualify our determination to make our own decisions by rising above the letter of the law in obedience to its spirit.

As to the second question regarding the upbringing of my own children, we do, of course, have rules at our house. I do not believe we would survive twenty-four hours without them. But that is not the point. The point with regard to learning to make one's own decisions does not have to do with whether or not there are rules. It has to do with how the rules are presented to a child and how he learns to relate them. Are the rules presented to a child in such a way that they point beyond themselves to their own rationale? Or are the rules presented as unquestionable absolutes?

One way to answer such questions is to look at what happens when a child breaks the rules. What is the parental response? And what message does it communicate to a child about the relative authority or sacredness of the rules? Does one respond simply to the breaking of the rule itself (which is easy to do when the parent's ego as rule giver is identified with the rule)? Or does one ask for and respond to the reason for which (the spirit in which) the rule was broken? The latter provides an opportunity to *learn* the rationale for the rule itself. It also provides an opportunity to learn what may be more important—that *in some situations* the rule may need to be broken in the name of its own rationale, and that one is respected for doing this. Of course, to assume this kind of responsibility as a parent is also to assume the responsibility to be honest about the rationales behind your rules. And that is not always easy. After all, sometimes the rationale is primarily a self-interest we are embarrassed to acknowledge. No one achieves the ideal in this realm, then. But it is this kind of ideal toward which I aspire in helping my own children to grow into responsible decision makers.

The key ingredient in such moral education is probably the amount of trust and affirmation communicated from the rule giver to the child who perceives himself as governed. If we treat our children as if they are responsible—by taking their motives and rationales seriously—they will probably learn to be responsible. The goal of moral education, then, and my goal as a parent, is to evoke in the child such a sense of trust in his own good judgment that he will be genuinely open to life's situations as he encounters them. This openness requires that he learn to trust his own perceptions, to affirm himself as a decision maker, to respect his own ideals, and not to fear the consequences of following them.

That is a big order. But then that full humanity in which one authentically decides for himself is also a big order. Some of us believe it is such a worthwhile dream for our children that it is worth running some of the apparent risks involved.

believing is not enough

A FRESHMAN COMPLAINS that she is "losing" her "faith" because
she simply "can't believe all those things anymore." A young
atheist proclaims: "I don't believe in any religion. I just have faith
in mankind." Another, calling himself an agnostic, responds: "I don't
have a faith. How can you have a faith in something that can't be
proved? I believe in following the Golden Rule."

Three sincere churchgoers, each considering himself a man of faith,
stand next to one another as they sing "Faith of Our Fathers." One
conjures up an image of the immutable creeds of the Church,
handed down from generation to generation. Another is thinking of
the continuity of the liturgy, "the faith" practiced and expressed in
the same words and rituals, perhaps even the same building, down
through the ages. The third contemplates the courage and confidence
of the pioneer spirit—faith meeting obstacles and overcoming fear.

FAITH AS RESPONSE

Faith is probably one of the most seriously misunderstood words
in the theologian's vocabulary. Therefore, any attempt to set forth
faith as a style of life needs to clarify this important word.

The best nontheological synonym for faith is *response*. Faith is
response. Faith is a way of responding to the world and one's experience of it. A particular man's faith includes the form and the

content of his response to what he perceives to be ultimately important for him. Faith is thus a bigger category than intellectual belief. It is also a bigger category than emotionality or the way I "feel" about myself. But faith includes all three: belief, behavior, emotion. Faith as response is all-inclusive, incorporating every mode of a man's being.[1]

Consequently, to say that you have faith in someone or something is to say that you respond in a total way. To have faith in Christ is to respond to Christ in a total way. One responds to him in a way which has many implications—for what he believes about himself and the world; for the decisions he makes; for how he experiences himself. Faith in God is essentially the same thing. However, since God is more abstract than Christ, and because for the Christian, God remains contentless without the figure of Christ, it is clearer to speak of faith in God only in terms of what is *revealed in Christ*.

It is possible, for example, to have faith in one's wife. That means more than considering one's wife a trustworthy person. To have faith in your wife is to respond to her in a more or less total way. This response includes what you believe about her, and about your relationship. It has clear implications for how one "ought" to behave toward his wife. And this response also includes one's feelings about himself. For example, in relationship to a lover we perceive ourselves as lovable persons. Like all analogies, this one breaks down at the point where there is a difference between faith in Christ and faith in one's wife. The latter does not have the character of absoluteness which marks a faith-response to Christ.

To say that faith is simply response, however, is inadequate. This response must be qualified by two adjectives which point to the uniqueness of the faith-response among other responses. One of these, *ultimate,* has already been mentioned. The other is *dynamic.*[2]

To say that faith's response is ultimate is more than simply to distinguish between faith in Christ and faith in other persons. It is to say something important about the object of faith. That in which I have faith is seen as ultimate, absolute, all-important for me. The object of faith is perceived as controlling my life. Loyalty to it ("Him") takes precedence over all other loyalties, personal or impersonal.

To recognize the ultimate nature of faith is also to recognize its essential subjectivity. To say that a person (or, in the case of Christ, a figure in a story) is ultimate is to make a statement which must always be qualified by "for me." To say that Christ is ultimate is to make a judgment about him, the truth of which cannot be demonstrated in any "objective" way. To try to make such a judgment objective or universal, as Christendom from time to time has done, is to destroy the meaning of words like *ultimate* and *absolute*. They are always dependent on the judgment of a responding subject. And such objectification of faith makes God (the final object of faith) absurdly objective. This can only confuse theological discourse and cause some men of faith to affirm the death of God. Its subjectivity then is essential to an understanding of faith. It has been celebrated by Sören Kierkegaard and a few who have followed him, but largely ignored by many otherwise responsible theologians.

The other adjective by which faith's response needs to be qualified is *dynamic*. This is a difficult word to define. Its root is a Greek word (*dunamis*) meaning "power," which appears in the New Testament describing the ministry of Jesus, his impact on others. To say that faith is dynamic is to say that it includes an element of power. The faith-response is powerful. Faith is a dynamic style of life. It is not merely passive, as when I respond (sometimes almost unconsciously) to the rhythm and beauty of the clouds drifting past my window. Faith's response enervates, activates, transforms, and empowers the responder. It is power.

When one is attracted by someone of the opposite sex or deeply stirred by another person, it is popular to say that you are "turned on." That is a good idiom for the experience of a dynamic response to another person. It has the effect of charging and energizing one. This is the sense in which faith is dynamic and faith's response is always a dynamic response. It turns you on. In the same way, political leaders or charismatic speakers can turn one on. This is experienced as power, not simply as diffuse excitement and exaggerated capacities as in some drug usage.

A faith-response, however, is not exclusively a response to other persons. Although a personal dimension remains, people respond in faith to events, myths, and stories. The normative instance of faith in the Bible is the response of a small band of Israelites to their exodus from Egypt. It is the response of a group of people to an event in their own history and to what they perceived to be happening in that event. The deliverance from bondage and the promise of a new life is fraught with ultimate meaning for the Israelites who experienced it. Their response says in effect: What has happened here has ultimate meaning for us as a community; leads us to believe that a force not of our own making has acted benevolently on our behalf; designates the values which shall govern our behavior; indicates the future goal and course of our corporate history; indicates how we shall view ourselves. Or, it says: The Lord God has brought us up out of Egypt in an act which we and our children must always remember; He has given us His law by which to live in a covenant relationship to Him; He has promised us a land flowing with milk and honey if we will but keep His covenant and serve Him; and He has made us His people.[3]

Of course, one need not witness an event in order for it to evoke a faith-response. It is possible to respond in faith to a story (even if the event did not occur as recorded) when one appropriates it as "his" story. Thus, countless generations of Jews and Christians have responded in faith to the Exodus story without participating in the historical crossing of the Red Sea. Such individuals often experience the Exodus in their own history (e.g., some personal deliverance from bondage or perception of the promise of a new life). They read their own experience through the Exodus story which has become their story. This reflects the sense in which every man of faith is a theologian. He interprets the event or story to which he responds. This has happened recently as American black men have rediscovered the relevance of the Exodus story to their own struggle.

That a story of an event can evoke faith as much as the event itself points up the mythological character of Holy Scripture in the Judeo-Christian tradition. To say that the Bible stories are myths is not to say that they are not true. On the contrary, it is to say that they are eminently true. They reveal that which is ulimately true for one who responds to them in faith. The proper understanding of myth is "a story about the Gods," i.e., a story about what is ultimately important. Because Bible stories are myths, their truth is not dependent on historical or empirical verification. Their truth is of another order. They are true because they are true for someone. They accurately describe his life as he experiences it. And insofar as these are his stories, they may also influence the way he experiences his life. In Malcolm X's *Autobiography*,[4] the author recounts how Muslim ideology and mythology converted him because it jibed with his experience. And in turn it provided him with a new way of interpreting his experience and a new imperative to action. The result was that he appeared to his former friends a different person—a man reborn.

Therefore, it does not matter to the man of faith whether or not the biblical stories occurred as they are recorded. What matters is the truth they hold for him and that it is an ultimate truth. What matters is that they evoke from him a faith-response. He may also respond, for example, to the truth about his existence dramatized in the story of Hamlet. But this response is not dependent on the historical accuracy of the Hamlet story. Likewise, Sigmund Freud responded to the Oedipus myth, but he certainly never assumed it to be historically accurate in the ordinary sense.[5]

Faith as response is then different from belief. The failure to distinguish between the two underlies much of the confusion about faith in the Church today. This is because the tendency to equate faith with belief reduces faith to an intellectual exercise. With regard to the stories of the Bible, one may believe that a story is historically accurate for a number of reasons. They would reflect historical scholarship and the ways in which one has learned to read and evaluate history. But because one believes a story to be historically accurate (e.g., that the Israelites did walk through the Red Sea), he does not necessarily respond to it in faith. Likewise, a genuine faith-response is not dependent on belief that the story occurred as recorded.

For example, I happen to believe that Jesus really lived. I believe this not because of my Christian faith, but rather on the basis of historical and biblical scholarship and the ways in which I have learned to be discriminating about past events. However, it does not make any difference to my Christian faith whether he lived or not. What is important is the way in which the story informs and describes my life. What is important is faith, not belief. And in this case, the two appear to be quite independent of one another. I do not need to believe that certain things happened a long time ago in order to have faith. Neither do I need to have faith in order to make reasonable judgments about the historicity of Bible stories. Those judgments are made on the basis of the highest degree of probability, using all the tools of research at my disposal.[6] The American Negro who responds to the Exodus story today probably does not care whether it really happened that way. The story has power for him nevertheless. It is *his* story.

The college student whose faith is shaken by evidence which questions the accuracy of some Bible stories probably never had a meaningful faith. Faith has been confused with belief. And the undercutting of certain naïve historical beliefs may be a great step forward. It is often the first step on the road to a meaningful personal faith—one which comprehends a whole style of life.

A colleague reports that when young people lament that their education has caused them to lose their faith, they are saying that they have lost not *their* faith but someone else's beliefs. And the time is now ripe for them to build a meaningful faith, one not constricted by parental beliefs.

A similar distinction may be made between faith and religion. Following Bonhoeffer's concept of "religionless Christianity," [7] Christianity is not a religion but a faith.[8] The essence of Christianity is the dynamic and ultimate response called faith, not intellectual assent to doctrines. Religion here is beliefs and practices derived from the hypothesis that a supreme being exists. A religious man is one who holds certain beliefs or indulges in certain practices (e.g., formal worship) related to this hypothesis. When this distinction is made, it becomes clear that one need not be religious in order to have faith. Neither need one be a man of faith in order to be religious. More widespread recognition of this distinction could be an important step in the renewal of the Church in our time.

A distinguished preacher once commented after a campus visit on how many atheists there were in the ostensibly religious group he had met. He was referring to those who confused faith with religion. They appeared long on religious beliefs and activities, short on a meaningful and integrative faith. Perhaps their only real faith was in the efficacy of certain rituals. This is a form of atheism. It is essentially anti-God and anti-faith. It replaces the Ultimate with weak substitutes and puts the emphasis on being religious rather than faithful. Specific acts rather than a whole style become most important.

Defining faith as response leads to a new recognition of the universality of faith. If faith is man's response to what is ultimate for him, every man has a faith. Every man is ultimately concerned about something, even if it is himself. Every man has a "god." With such an understanding, the possibility of a multiplicity of faiths must also be recognized. Faith is universal only as long as one does not limit the criteria of faith according to his own religion. To do this is an insult to the atheist who is not a man of faith where faith is circumscribed by the forms of another's religiosity (e.g., the figure of Jesus, the life of the Church, etc.). To tell an atheist he has a "god" when *God* has already been limited by a religious tradition is not to listen seriously to what his faith really is. The recognition of the universality of faith then should not keep churchmen from listening to apparent nonbelievers in a time when listening seems particularly urgent for the Church.

BELIEF AS INTELLECTUAL ASSENT

In spite of the distinction between faith and belief—faith incorporates belief. Belief, like morality, is one expression of faith. On the basis of his faith, a man comes to believe certain things about himself, his God, and his world. But belief alone is not enough. Belief must be grounded in faith. Otherwise, it becomes irrelevant metaphysical speculation.

In this sense, belief is the intellectual expression of faith. It is the affirmation which grows out of a man's faith-response. Belief follows faith; faith does not follow belief. When intellectual assent to doctrine is made a precondition of faith, the Church fails to distinguish between faith and belief, and distorts its own message.

Belief is the cognitive superstructure which men erect on the foundations of faith. Where faith is response, belief is making sense out of that response. Thus, creedal statements are attempts by the Church in a particular time and place to systematize her faith and make it understandable to herself and communicable to others. Consequently, creeds are always relative to the historical context which produced them. To absolutize creeds as if intellectual submission were a precondition to faith is to misunderstand creeds and the nature of religious belief. It also usually sets up unnecessary roadblocks to faith.

If religious belief is the superstructure of faith, the forms of belief should be in continuous need of revision. A proposition which expressed the faith of a sixteenth-century reformer may be simply inappropriate in the cultural and intellectual climate of the twentieth century. And statements of belief acceptable in the intellectual milieu of the fourth century, and addressed specifically to issues of that time, may be quite inappropriate expressions of faith for a twentieth-century man. Likewise, contemporary thought categories used in this book may be just as inappropriate and meaningless for a man of faith in the twenty-first century. It would be as arrogant to impose our forms of belief on him as it is to impose fourth-century forms on us. Such attempts usually drive away from the Church those who might otherwise express their faith through her forms. They imperil the intellectual respectability of Christian belief. And they require of honest men within the Church intellectual gymnastics which render their faith virtually incommunicable to others.

For example, when a man and woman fall in love they hold beliefs about one another which they will subsequently say were unrealistic. But those beliefs (e.g., that the other is always gentle or soft-spoken) were nonetheless appropriate at the time. The faith which evokes those beliefs will remain substantially the same over many years. It will even deepen as beliefs about one another are adjusted to fit the data of experience. The form of such belief must be constantly revised in order for faith or love to remain alive and contemporary. In marriages where this does not happen, individuals become dissatisfied because the other partner fails to conform to an earlier belief or image. Love atrophies when it is tied to an outmoded belief about the other person. Likewise, faith atrophies when it is tied to an outmoded belief about God.

Is there, then, any value to creedal statements? This again questions the usefulness of a contemporary statement of faith which may change. The answer is that statements of belief are absolutely necessary, for groups as well as for individuals. We must constantly be about the business of "making sense" out of our faith-response, both for our own self-understanding and for purposes of communication. A meaningful faith can no more survive without intellectual superstructure (however tentative) than a love relationship can survive without beliefs (however tentative) about the beloved.

Should creeds or other statements of belief then be discarded when they seem historically dated? No. They are instructive and helpful in teaching us how our faith has been interpreted and articulated in other times and situations. Indeed, they are an indispensable part of the tradition through which we make our faith-response. But they are not absolute, unquestionable statements. And they should never be treated as such. They are important guidelines and forms to which me must pay heed, but also "sit loosely." The point of view of this book, for example, is deeply informed by the creedal formulations of the Council of Nicaea, but it is not bound to them.

Finally, religious belief provides a meaningful frame of reference for faith. This is another way of understanding belief as intellectual assent and as superstructure. Everyone holds some frame of reference within which he views reality. It is in part a product of his experience and in part consists of beliefs accepted uncritically from parents and other authority figures. A child who has been stung believes because of his experience that bees are painful, bad, and dangerous. But a child who has been told by his parents that bees should be avoided, or who has observed his parents in the presence of bees, will likewise believe that bees are painful, bad, and dangerous. Such beliefs are part of a frame of reference and influence the way one responds to reality, e.g., the reality of a bee sitting on his arm.

Likewise, religious beliefs represent faith's frame of reference. They even influence the ongoing nature of faith. To respond, for example, to Jesus by affirming that he represents what is ultimately important, is to make a primitive statement of belief. One has begun to articulate a frame of reference for his faith. He may now refine it with more concrete beliefs, such as that Jesus is the Son of God. This belief was once apparently an appropriate expression of Christian faith. For many today it does not fit comfortably in a modern frame of reference. It is an inadequate expression of faith. So honest men of faith avoid it, preferring to say that the relationship of Jesus to God is that Jesus reveals the nature of God (a rather orthodox statement, incidentally, for which there are good biblical precedents).[9] Here, religious belief is informed by a total frame of reference and becomes its religious dimension. The "modern" frame of reference influences the form of faith's expression. Because one is not hung up by the Son of God idea, he is free to respond to Jesus in ways which might be closed if he had to believe in the kind of supernatural being which "Son of God" suggests to the twentieth-century mind. Consequently, belief as the intellectual frame of reference of faith, like any superstructure, puts pressure on its foundation. (Part of the problem here is that the phrase "Son of God," like the traditional understanding of the Virgin Birth, implies biological/physiological origins. This invokes an outmoded metaphysic, and contradicts the best insights of modern science and technology. Even if the Virgin Birth could be empirically verified, the doctrine would not persuade one that Jesus reveals God. Like other biblical mythology, the nativity accounts in the New Testament have their roots in primitive legend which predates Jesus. They are metaphorical expressions of the faith that Jesus reveals the fullness of God, just as a son reveals the nature of his father.)

THE NONEXISTENCE OF GOD

What then of the object of faith? This is the reality men call God. The word *reality* avoids use of the word *being* in regard to God. If God is initially defined as a being, the issue concerning the object of faith has already been circumscribed by a particular understanding of God.

There is a problem of language here because even *reality* prejudices the case. Any synonym for God betrays some religious tradition, shows some preconceptions concerning the nature of God. *Reality* seems preferable in contemporary usage because it is more abstract, more ambiguous, and less "loaded" than *being* or *person,* two popular alternatives.

The central question is: What kind of reality is God? What image does the word *God* evoke in the mind of the man of faith? To what data of his own experience does he appeal when he uses this word?

Traditionally, *God* has been assumed by believers and nonbelievers to refer to a discrete being with the properties of existence in time and space. The most popular image in the Judeo-Christian tradition has been a person. Indeed, the properties often ascribed to this being (omnipotence, omniscience, etc.) are borrowed from the realm of interpersonal experience. They convey a personal image. Thus, God becomes a personlike being, whose properties transcend or extend the usual limitations of personhood, and who clearly exists (where existence means discrete being under the conditions of time and space).[10] In the Bible, this being thinks, makes plans, has personlike emotions, acts, and reacts. "He" exercises absolute and arbitrary control over the course of history and the processes of nature.

However, in the same biblical record, God is never seen, heard or otherwise sensually perceived *qua being* except under the cover of a natural or historical symbol. In the Old Testament, He is perceived acting in the Exodus, "seen" in a burning bush and in pillars of cloud and fire, "heard" as a still, small voice, and experienced as an overwhelming presence in certain visionary experiences. Indeed, it is explicitly understood that no man can see God's face and live. And concrete images or representations are prohibited by God Himself. Likewise, in the New Testament, this being is beyond ordinary sensual perception except insofar as "His" fullness is revealed in the life of one man.

The Bible, then, assumes the existence of an object of faith. This is, however, not demonstrable in the way in which the existence of a table or an historical person is demonstrable. The existence of this supreme being is less concrete. Thus, even in the biblical narrative, the meaning of *existence* is being stretched when it is applied to God.

In the same biblical record, God is also understood as "spirit," "love," and "truth." In what sense do spirit, love, and truth exist? Certainly not as discernible and demonstrable to the human senses. To say that love, for example, exists in a way that one can localize and temporize it, "capture" it and show it, is to reduce the meaning of *love*. Likewise, it is playing loose with language to say that love is a being (although it might be meaningful to say that love is a quality of being or "Being itself").[11] In contemporary usage it is linguistically more responsible to say that love is a reality. This reality men experience in relationship to one another. Likewise, spirit, truth, and beauty are experienced by men in relationship. They are abstractions which defy any definition that would make them into discrete and identifiable beings.

Each of these "realities" has about it a strong element of subjectivity. Beauty *is* in the eye of the beholder. The concepts of love and truth are meaningless without the existence of individuals who experience love and truth in relationship. Beauty, for example, is a judgment made by a subject in his relationship to something or someone else that exists. The beauty of the sunset can be no more demonstrated or verified than can one's love for his wife or the meaning which he finds in his existence. Indeed, there are people who for good cause might find the sunset ugly, another's wife unlovable, and existence meaningless and absurd. It is more appropriate, therefore, to speak of beauty, love, and truth as "qualities of experience" or "realities" of life, than to call them "beings." Indeed, it would never occur to most of us to speak of love as a being, or a supreme being, even when love is the supremely important reality in our lives.

Popular usage of the word *God* is similar. Is it then legitimate to speak of the "existence" of a supreme being or an object of faith? To say that God exists in a way that I can localize and temporize His being is to reduce the meaning of *God*. It makes God less than God. We have seen that there are biblical injunctions against such idolatry, against making any graven image of God. Therefore, most of the traditional talk about the existence of God is idolatrous and anti-God. It reduces Him to what Tillich calls "a being among other beings." God becomes one of the neighbors. When this happens, serious theologians feel called to affirm the nonexistence of God.[12] It is misleading to say that God is a being. It is more accurate to say that God is a reality which men experience in relationship to one another. And that corresponds to the biblical understanding that God acts in history. One has simply reduced the anthropomorphism of the biblical view in a way which makes it more understandable to the twentieth-century mind. The statement "God acts in history" is equivalent to the proposition that God is that ultimate reality which men perceive operating and directing the dynamics of human relationships, i.e., making history. For twentieth-century man, science and technology have extensively defined and explored the world of concrete things. Therefore, he needs all the more to acknowledge how gross an abstraction *God* is. In order to maintain a meaningful relationship to God, he needs to acknowledge the nonexistence of God.

This kind of usage highlights the subjectivity of faith. Kierkegaard's dictum that "Truth is Subjectivity" [13] (where God, for Kierkegaard, is Truth) amounts to saying that God is in the eye of the beholder. The concept of God is meaningless without individuals who experience God in their history, their relationships. Even in the Bible, the concept of God presupposes subjects who respond to Him in faith. The normative experience of God in the Bible, the Exodus, presupposes a group of people involved in the dynamics of history. We should not forget that the Egyptians were allegedly also at the Red Sea, and apparently went away with quite another impression of what had happened. Likewise, whatever the Resurrection accounts mean, it is clear from the biblical record that not all present had this experience. There is an inescapable dimension of subjectivity to the normative Christian faith-response. To say that God is in Christ is to say that God is in Christ "for me," because that is the way one experiences and responds to the figure of Christ. He is the embodiment of that which is ultimate (for me).

Such an understanding of God raises problems with language. These are at the root of so-called "death of God" theology. A Church which thinks of God as a being has understandable difficulty grasping the underlying biblical motif of the nonexistence of God. Indeed, such talk sounds at best heretical, and often blasphemous, anti-God, and atheistic. Ironically, those who proclaim the death or nonexistence of God consider language about His existence itself to be blasphemous, anti-God, and atheistic! For them, "death of God" talk is an affirmation of God *qua* reality.

How then can an object of faith who is simply a perceived reality be the active agent portrayed in the biblical record? How can such a God think? How can he make plans for his world? How can he hear prayers? How can he respond to the actions and desires of men? How can he intervene at his own whim in the course of history and the processes of nature? These questions are posed most frequently in two forms: How can a God who does not exist be the Creator of the universe? What about the God of whom Jesus spoke as a Father, and to whom he prayed?

Such questions reveal genuine perplexity. They must be received as sincere attempts to be true to the biblical tradition. However, they are based on at least two debatable assumptions. First, they assume that a God who is understood as a nonexistent reality must be passive. Although understandable, that assumption is not defensible. Let us return to the love analogy.[14] To say that love is a reality to which one responds in relationship is not to say that love is inactive. Our experience of love is usually quite the contrary, notably that love is dynamic, that love is powerful, that love *is* power. Love has the power to stir one to action. Indeed, it appears to have the power to stir men to acts of which they would otherwise be incapable.

In addition, love is experienced as a reality which is "there" whether or not one recognizes it. Even when love is not perceived, it may still characterize a relationship. Love is nonetheless real if one is unable or unwilling to acknowledge it. For example, a person may act in a self-sacrificial way which, because of my obtuseness (or what in the Bible is called "hardness of heart") I fail to respond to as love. One may even misinterpret an act as the opposite of love. But love has been nonetheless active in a relationship. And there is no telling what the effect of its activity on the actor has been. The "activity" of God is similar. Hence, the assumption that a nonexistent God is an inactive God is untenable. He is no more incapable of action than are love, beauty, and truth. All of them have generated considerable effect in the course of human history.

The activity of such a God is, however, not purely self-initiated. Like the activity of love, it is dependent on the actions of existing individuals. Although love is experienced as coming from outside the self and evoking response, love acts on us through an agent, another person. Consequently, to speak of the activity of God in history as if it were not dependent on the agency of men is to use a metaphor which cannot be literalized. When it is, it contradicts the biblical understanding that God selects a people to be his agents in history. This means that individuals and communities experience themselves as "chosen" (to a particular task in history) by a reality greater than themselves. Such an understanding of divine activity undercuts the concept of a purely self-initiating God. But the God who is undercut is foreign to the biblical narrative where God is understood as standing in a covenant relationship to man.

A second debatable assumption is that the literary forms, metaphors, and idioms of the biblical writers are eternally valid and literally accurate. This fails to make an adequate distinction between faith and belief. Faith becomes equated with intellectual assent to the beliefs of men who lived two thousand years ago. Because of the discrepancy between the world views of the biblical writers and our present age, that is a tenuous equation. In addition, absolutizing biblical metaphors ignores the biblical narrative itself. There is considerable development and change in the understanding of God from the Mosaic period to the later New Testament writers. And Jesus was reportedly considered a blasphemer for raising some knotty problems with the understanding of God and "His" activity which was prevalent in his time.[15] The rejection of an understanding of God because it does not conform to certain biblical metaphors (e.g., God "hearing" prayers, "feeling" anger, "sending" messengers) is then untenable on the grounds of scripture itself. It is true that the biblical writers did not speak of the nonexistence of God. Their metaphors assumed an object of faith who was a discrete being in time and space. But their view of reality was neither informed nor troubled by science, technology, historical scholarship, and corresponding revolutions in the objective and subjective worlds of human experience.

For these reasons, modern man appears to need a "spirit-centered" theology. If a theology represents an "understanding of God" (the *logos* of the *theos*), then a "spirit-centered" theology understands God primarily under the heading of spirit. Because the concept of spirit is biblical and theologically traditional, to speak of God as spirit is less shocking to religious sensitivities than to speak of a nonexistent reality. The two, however, mean essentially the same thing.[16] From the first Creation myth to the post-Resurrection gift of the Holy Spirit, God is consistently understood in the Bible as "spiritual." [17] (The proper meaning of the word *spiritual* is "having the qualities of spirit," not "spooky," "ghostly," or "otherworldly" as the word has come to be misused in some religious jargon.) Like love, beauty, and truth, spirit is intangible. A spirit cannot be isolated. It cannot be localized or temporized in an identifiable and demonstrable way. A spirit is pervasive in ways that suggest traditional attributes of the deity, e.g., omnipresence.

The word *spirit,* like other good theological terms, is borrowed from the realm of everyday human experience (what is sometimes called the "secular").[18] There is, for example, a spirit of America. Americans participate in it and experience it as a reality of life. Although awareness of this spirit is often more acute when we are in the presence of other Americans and self-conscious of the spirit which binds us together, this spirit is not limited to the history of the American nation. Neither is it limited to American geography or even to people who are Americans. This spirit is free and "bloweth where it will." The spirit of America need not be the ultimate spirit in one's life to be a reality and to enervate and stimulate one to action. One nonetheless responds to this spirit in a way which informs his beliefs, his actions, and his feelings. The same is true of the spirit of a college alma mater. This "secular" spirit has to do with self-conscious membership in a community of people with shared experiences. And a college spirit can often be evoked by ritualistic, ceremonial occasions (like college reunions).

To propose a spirit-centered theology, to say that God is spirit,

is to say of the object of faith all of these things and more. It is to
say that God is that spirit which is ultimate in one's life. He is that
spirit which transcends all other spirits and loyalties and binds them
together. When the spirit of America is worth serving, for example,
it is because of compatibility with the spirit one calls God. And
when the spirit of America seems incompatible with one's God/
spirit, then many men of faith either reject or criticize the spirit of
America.

An understanding of God as spirit is at the heart of the doctrine
of the Trinity, in spite of the intellectual difficulties which that
doctrine occasions for twentieth-century man. In addition to its
polemic against heresies prevalent in the early Church, trinitarian
thinking asserts that Christian faith begins with an experience of
God as spirit. It is only necessary to speak of a threefold nature of
God when He is encountered essentially as spirit. If we continue to
think of the godhead in terms of three persons (and it is not clear,
as Bishop Pike has pointed out,[19] that the doctrine is any longer a
helpful statement of belief), then contemporary theology should
establish the Holy Spirit as *the* important "person" from the experiential perspective of faith. The other two persons (Son and Father)
are needed because spirit remains amorphous until given form by
an historical personage. Therefore, an affirmation of the Holy Spirit
points (for the Christian) to the figure of Jesus of Nazareth, who
defines that spirit. Likewise, Jesus is portrayed and encountered as
always pointing beyond himself. He is not God. If he were, he would
become an idol, as some non-Christians fear he is. He remains a
fully human man whose uniqueness lies in his revealing to the eyes of
faith the fullness of God. Consequently, if the Trinity is to be rescued
for contemporary man, it may need to be read backwards, i.e., Spirit,
Son and Father.[20]

THE NEED FOR A MEDIUM

Because *spirit* is amorphous, it remains useless to theological discourse without a concrete referent. This gives it form. The word
spirit is as great an abstraction as the word *God*. It demands definition. As both words have been used here, there are actually many
spirits and many gods. When one speaks of a spirit which is ultimate
for him (a Holy Spirit), it behooves him to identify its properties.

Just as the spirit of America and the spirit of one's college alma mater remain amorphous without the existence of America and the college, so the God/spirit remains "hidden" without a concrete historical event or person.

There is therefore a need for a medium in any spirit-centered theology. To become a reality in one's life, spirit must be detected under the cover of some concrete form. This form functions as a mediator. It stands between one and the spirit to which he responds. And it is the basis of their relationship. For the Christian, this medium has traditionally been the personage of Jesus of Nazareth. To say that Jesus reveals the nature of God or that "God was in Christ" is to say that Jesus functions as a mediator of the spirit to which faith responds. The Christian answer to questions concerning the nature of God is to point to Jesus and say: That is what God is like. That is the record (the New Testament) of the operation of the spirit which is ultimate for me. (For the Christian, of course, the Old Testament is a record of the operation of the same spirit. But the Christian recognizes this only after-the-fact of his confrontation with the concrete personal medium of Jesus. This confrontation is in turn meaningless without the Old Testament. The view of history and God revealed in the New Testament presupposes the Old Testament narrative. Many New Testament stories have their prototypes in the history of the people of Israel. Jesus' own self-understanding is deeply informed by the Old Testament. At the same time, from the viewpoint of Christian faith, the spirit revealed throughout the Old Testament record takes on its most concrete and dynamic form in the New Testament. The Old Testament, for a Christian, comes alive because of the New Testament—although the reverse is also true.)

This does not mean there can be no spirit-centered theology without Jesus. Neither does it claim that Jesus is in any objective sense a better or more effective medium than others. It means only that from a Christian perspective, Jesus is *the* medium who gives form and substance to the reality called God. That is what makes the Christian faith-response "Christian." The object of faith is focused in the person of Jesus Christ. A Christian can and will respond to other mediators of the same spirit, but only because of and as defined by Jesus. For example, one can read the biography of Mahatma Gandhi and respond with genuine excitement to the spirit revealed therein as the spirit of Christ.[21] But one does not thereby become a

Gandhian. Gandhi does not replace Christ as *the* medium for the God/spirit. One responds to Gandhi's story and says: *There* is God (or the spirit of Christ) operating in history. Gandhi is responded to against the background of the form provided by Jesus. This does not make Gandhi a Christian. That would be historically inaccurate and presumptuous toward the way in which Gandhi apparently perceived his own commitments. Insofar as Jesus was not for Gandhi *the* medium of the God/spirit, Gandhi was not a Christian. This is true in spite of his being one of the more Christlike figures in history. To make Gandhi or other loving and self-giving persons into Christians simply on the basis of their behavior reduces faith to ethics and confuses the meaning of the word *Christian*. It undercuts the sense in which a particular medium defines any spirit which is perceived as universal. And it is the nature of the medium which distinguishes one faith from another, even when the spirits responded to have much in common.

The need for a medium is at the heart of so-called sacramental theology. In spite of the broad disrepute into which sacramental thinking has fallen, particularly within Protestantism, the Christian faith-response remains essentially sacramental. Christian faith presupposes and depends upon outward forms, the norm for all of which is Jesus of Nazareth. Traditionally, a sacrament is "an outward and visible sign of an inward and spiritual Grace." [22] A sacrament is any concrete form (a person, an event, a story) which reveals that spirit which is ultimate and essentially intangible. The phrase "inward and spiritual Grace" points up, among other things, the subjectivity of faith.

The problem with sacramental thinking, and the reason that it has been theologically suspect (e.g., Old Testament warnings against graven images illustrate an early recognition of the dangers of "sacramentalism"), is the tendency to equate form with content, to forget that God is spirit, and to make the medium itself the object of faith. Because of the boldness which identifies a person as the revealer of God, Christianity is more subject to this tendency than Judaism. (Although Judaism does not identify itself as a sacramental faith, it practices a qualified sacramentalism insofar as particular historical events are viewed as revealing God. And if there is a modified tendency to fall into the same abuse within Judaism, it is the failure to distinguish between the form of an event and the reality revealed, leading to what might be called "historiolatry.")

Because sacramental thinking holds that any form may reveal the Spirit (since one form—Jesus—does), we should probably speak in terms of a sacramental "view of life" rather than a sacramental theology. The phrase "sacramental theology" implies that *sacramental* has to do only with practices and objects which are identified as "religious." They are somehow separated or different from the common (secular) world. When one catalogs as sacraments certain "religious" practices he will tend to ignore the sacramental nature (i.e., potential for revealing the Spirit) of everything that exists. Then those practices and objects which are designated as sacramental become removed from the world of real life where the Spirit is encountered, become fraught with all kinds of magical connotations, and ultimately become objects of veneration themselves. This is idolatry, a denial of God against which the Bible repeatedly warns.

Consequently, it is proper to speak of particular sacraments only within a sacramental view of life. This allows the man of faith to affirm the need for a medium without limiting the medium to certain man-made acts, rituals, and objects. Of course, when one speaks of a spirit defined by its medium, one has limited that spirit by its definition. However, the man of faith does not need to compound this limitation by further constriction of his normative medium. The maximum affirmation of a sacramental view of life, from a Christian perspective, is: Because Jesus is sacrament, all of life, from Gandhi to yesterday's sunset, is potentially sacramental. Certain traditional practices of the Church are sacramental only insofar as participation in them genuinely mediates the spirit of Christ. My participation in the Communion meal on one occasion might be sacramental. On another, it might be blasphemous or idolatrous, or both. With a sacramental view of life, the essential subjectivity of faith cannot be discounted.

A sacramental world view opens the possibility of a variety of mediators of the same spirit. That Jesus is *the* medium for one gives no cause for arrogance toward those whose central "sacrament" is another form. The task of the man of faith vis-à-vis those of another faith is neither to reject nor to disregard, but rather to listen. If a faith-response fills one's life with meaning and purpose and pervades every aspect of his being, he should feel no threat from a faith-response which assumes a different form. He will also desire to share with others the "good news" of his faith, that it transforms his existence, that it becomes his style of life. One cannot communicate this unless he listens. And when he listens, he may learn that the form of another man's faith mediates the spirit of his own faith. Because forms differ, he may also learn new dimensions of his spirit/God. Although Jesus may reveal the fullness of God, Christian faith is always perceived as incomplete, as in a constant state of unfolding and becoming. And the only difference between faiths may finally be one of form, of what is *the* medium for the same spirit, the same life-style. A Christian need not feel any imperative to alter the form of another's faith (or to attack his medium), but only the responsibility to expose him to the form of his own faith-response. This is Christian witness. It is at the heart of the missionary nature of Christianity. The mission is, however, misunderstood when spirit is confused with form, when the forms of other faiths are not listened to seriously, and when culturally and historically relative beliefs and practices are imposed (through coercion, persuasion, or bribery) on those for whom they are inappropriate and inexpressive. (For a sensitive account of the potentially disastrous and sometimes ludicrous effects of this kind of missionary confusion, see James Michener, *Hawaii*.) Such imposition demonstrates that one has not yet learned that believing is not enough.

A few years ago a college chapel preacher gave a rather stirring presentation of the "existential" dimensions of Christian faith. He stressed the provision of meaning and purpose to an otherwise absurd existence. After the service a student told him that he agreed with everything he had said, but found it all in the writings of Albert Camus. He saw no reason to call himself a Christian in order to make these affirmations. The preacher asked: "Do you really find all that I said in Camus?"

"Yes."

"And do you really believe it with all your heart?"

"Yes."

"Well then, hallelujah! You find it in Camus and I find it in Jesus. Welcome to the club!"

There are, of course, other questions which could be asked, but the story illustrates openness to a variety of mediators. For some married folk, their mate is *the* medium for their experience of "married love." But no one assumes that everyone must be married to *his* wife in order to experience married love! And no one should assume that he cannot learn about love and his own marital relationship by listening to other lovers. When one perceives a kindred spirit, when he encounters another responding to the same spirit which he finds in his own love relationship, then the right response is: Hallelujah! And welcome to the club!

SPIRIT AND FORM

A central issue in the experience of faith is the problem of spirit and form. Where God is understood as spirit, and where the need for a medium is recognized, a tension is established between spirit and the form which reveals spirit on a given occasion. To attempt to resolve this tension by failing to distinguish between spirit and form leads to idolatry. Therefore, as long as the object of faith remains abstract (spirit) but dependent on that which is concrete (form), faith is paradoxical. Faith affirms two "truths" which appear to be contradictory but are nonetheless valid. For example, the Christian affirms a paradox when he says that God is spirit and that Jesus reveals the fullness of God. Or: God is eternal and universal, beyond the conditions of time and space, but God is only revealed under the conditions of particular time and space. Or, as Kierkegaard puts it, the ultimate paradox of Christian faith is that the eternal is revealed in time.[23] The spirit which is eternal "breaks into" history.

Because of the paradoxical nature of faith, all statements of belief are relative to the conditions under which they are made. This explains the antipathy of Kierkegaard and others to theological systems or any attempt to solidify belief. It also justifies the traditional Hebraic suspicion of doctrinal thinking. Where God is revealed in the dynamics of history, "He" cannot be captured or exhausted within any particular doctrinal formulation. The man of faith must therefore maintain the unabsoluteness of any form, except in the "moment" of revelation. No form (event, person, story) is absolute, although in the "moment" in which it reveals the ultimate spirit a form itself is experienced as ultimate.

For Christians, this extends even to the form which is Jesus. Theologians generally avoid this extension because it implies a thoroughgoing theological relativism. Its value, on the other hand, is that it underscores the full humanity of Jesus. He was a man *in all respects*. Although orthodox, such statements shock many churchmen because the Church tends to venerate Jesus. It makes him an object of faith rather than a mediator. (The same tendency is evident in Roman Catholic treatment of Mary. According to orthodox thinking, she is to be understood as a mediatrix. But often in Catholic iconography and practice, she becomes an object of faith.) Where Jesus becomes an object of faith, Christianity degenerates into Jesusolatry, veneration of a dead hero. This is a denial of the Resurrection (see Chapter 1) as a present reality. It also makes Christianity idolatrous. It leads to the unfortunate by-products of idolatry: rigidity of thinking, conformity of behavior, and deadness of spirit. It also contradicts the teachings of Jesus himself ("Why do you call me good? No one is good but God alone" [24]). And it justifies Jewish charges that much Christian belief and practice has abandoned the essence of Judaism.

This, however, does not alter the absoluteness of the medium in the "moment" of the faith-response. When one recognizes in Jesus the fullness of God, Jesus in that moment becomes God. But this is not objective, static, or unchangeable. It is analogous to the way, in the ecstasy of love, the beloved (who is always "just" a mediator of love) becomes love itself. We respond in terms of endearment which, if taken literally, would be absurd.

The paradoxical nature of faith, then, implies the danger of idolatry. In both the biblical record and the dynamics of faith's experience, idolatry is *the* great enemy. Idolatry is "unfaith." It has all the earmarks of faith—subjectivity, ultimacy, dynamic power. But it is the exact opposite of faith because of a qualitative difference in the object of one's response. (Idolatry, incidentally, is closely related to sin, which can also be defined an unfaith; see Chapter 2.) Idolatry is making absolute that which by its nature is relative and conditioned. The worship *of* forms (rather than *through* forms) is idolatrous, as is the absolutizing of doctrinal beliefs, as is the absolutizing of any particular moral code (see Chapter 2). When we recognize the paradoxical nature of faith, when we see the inevitable tension between spirit and form, when we perceive that which is eternal and universal under the conditions of time and space, we should not be surprised that the risk of idolatry is the price we pay for a meaningful and relevant faith—one which represents an authentic and comprehensive style of life.

Perhaps the best safeguard against idolatry is built into the biblical faith-response itself. It is also the final criterion of biblical revelation —that the form falls away in the moment of revelation. A true medium becomes unimportant once it has done its job. It gets out of the way when its spirit becomes the object of faith. This criterion is, of course, transparently Christian. It is derived from one meaning of the Crucifixion/Resurrection. This is that Jesus must die in order for the ultimate reality to be fully available to men without the "interference" of the form. That is the Christian statement of and answer to the problem of spirit and form, as it relates to faith.

A PERSONAL NOTE

Because the Church has long equated faith with belief, a radical distinction between them is still distressing and confusing to many people. Those distressed and confused include "nonbelievers" as well as believers. Indeed, the kind of Christian atheism presented here is often upsetting to other atheists. Their negative and polemical reasons for atheism seem undercut.

In dialogue with those confused by the distinction between faith and belief, I find myself most often responding to one of two questions: (1) What are your own beliefs (at this moment)? And how integral are they to your faith? (2) What has been the role of formal religious beliefs in your development of a faith? What is the place of belief in your pilgrimage in faith?

Of course, the substance of my faith is what this book is all about. The major beliefs which express my Christianity make up the six separate chapters. I experience these beliefs in a constant state of flux. I am always finding new ways of expressing and formulating them. This is a function of my ongoing experience as a human being (my living in the world) which is constantly refining my beliefs about myself and the world. For example, some of the roles I play are terribly important in this. Becoming a husband challenged and changed some of my beliefs. Likewise with becoming a father, a grown-up child to my parents, a preacher, a teacher, a counselor, etc.

The state of flux in which my beliefs are held is also a function of listening to others—both face-to-face and via the printed word. Their beliefs influence mine. For example, discovering depth psychology has had a deep and lasting influence on what I believe. It has altered my perceptions of my own faith. As the footnotes in this book make clear, Sören Kierkegaard has influenced my understanding of my faith in ways that are irreversible but still open to change. As I listen to others in this way, I am always in a process of changing my language. I am finding new and (for me) more accurate ways of telling what is inside. It is always slightly distressing to change language in this way, particularly when one is questioning and even discarding religious language with hallowed associations. This, I think, is the real problem some very serious Roman Catholics have with changes in the Mass. But, in my experience, this openness to new language is absolutely essential. Without it, spiritual growth (growth in the Spirit) is difficult. I fully expect, for example, that the language of the psychedelic movement and the language of the new political left—both of which speak with authority to certain levels of my being—will become part of my theology. These languages influence the ways in which I articulate my faith in belief.

This leads to the second question regarding my own pilgrimage in faith. As far as I am aware, religious beliefs have played a very important part in this process. This includes beliefs which I now consider outmoded, naïve or meaningless. Within the framework of a certain set of religious beliefs (including the existence of God) I was moved to seek a seminary education. I entered upon that experience with answers that I now find inadequate and with questions that now seem either answered or irrelevant. For example, at one point in my life I considered it very important to decide whether or not I believed that Mary was a virgin. That question now seems to me irrelevant and trivial, and my best guess is that she was not. At another point in my pilgrimage, I believed that I had found the vocational meaning of my life in service through the institutional Church. Experience has revised that "answer" and has called into question a number of other answers to the problem of meaning.

What then is the role of belief in this ongoing process of change? The best answer I can give is that belief is the base from which one changes his belief. That is paradoxical. Belief is that against which new ideas, new frames of reference, new languages, and ever-new experiences come up. Without such a base, I wonder if change or growth would be possible. I must know where I am in order to get to somewhere new. Religious belief at any given moment is "where I am" with my faith. But it must not become static or ossified into any particular form. That would deny the Spirit which undergirds belief and is always cropping out in new and unexpected forms. It would also deny me. I would cease to be alive and growing as a person, and would become dead and unchanging. I would cease to be process and would become static. That is a very threatening prospect for me.

One question remains to be addressed. When confronted with this kind of "process theology," some want to know what is left that is constant. Is there nothing then that is static, stable, unchangeable? This, of course, is what I have called faith. And again, faith is paradoxical. It is both changing and unchanging. Insofar as my beliefs (faith's frame of reference) change, my faith changes also, mostly in the direction of deepening and becoming more meaningful for me.

But, beneath all that change, there is something constant. You can call it God or you can call it my "inner Self." At one level, in spite of all the changes which have marked my own pilgrimage, I am the same person with the same basic values and problems and the same basic patterns of response to the world. Through faith, I am reborn to dizzy heights of self-awareness and self-transcendence. I am radically changed, but I still experience myself as the same person with the same God. That is a paradox.

My wife and I often ponder that in over fifteen years of married life we have each radically changed. And yet we also know that we are the same people we were when we married. This is, I think, the same paradox. It illustrates why flexibility in the forms of religious beliefs (in the name of their Spirit) is such an important dimension of my theology. It also illustrates why believing (the intellectual form of faith) simply is not enough.

4

being in community

ONE DOES NOT become faithful in a vacuum. A meaningful style of life is learned from the style of others. As long as God is spirit, and a medium is necessary, one medium of faith will be the personhood of others. Personhood expresses faith in all its ramifications—intellectual, ethical, emotional. This is particularly true where God, as in the biblical tradition, has a personal character. Then persons become the most significant mediators of the faith-response. Bishop Robinson uses this insight to point out that what was once perceived as man's search for a gracious God is today perceived as the search for a gracious neighbor.[1]

The social nature of faith leads to the emergence of the religious community. This is a group of people self-consciously bound together by a common faith-response. When its style of life is oriented around historical events, this community will also have a common history. In a pluralistic society the religious community appears as the religious establishment. The religious establishment is the institutionalized expression of communal faith. This is the Church. It is that institution which exists to perpetuate the faith—by preserving its traditions, practicing it, and communicating it to the world. Above all, it exists to serve its God. This is finally the only justification for the perpetuation of the religious establishment. Consequently, the religious community sees itself as "the people of God." It is the people called to be the corporate medium of its God to the world.

91

THE NEED FOR COMMUNITY

Is such a community necessary? If its function is to serve its God and proclaim its faith, could this not be done in a less self-conscious, more informal way? Is the complicated machinery of the religious establishment worth the energy it takes to keep it running?

Such questions are common in our time, from those within the Church as well as those outside. One should make a distinction here between the need for community *per se* and the need for any particular form of community. Because of the interpersonal nature of faith's response, some self-conscious communal life appears to be a *sine qua non* of biblical faith. It is not clear, however, that any particular form of this community is essential to faith. Indeed, the biblical mandate for this community calls for the breaking of its form, a continuous re-forming, an ongoing reformation. Like the "new" morality, the new reformation of which Bishop Robinson and others (e.g., Roger Lloyd, *op. cit.,* and Harvey Cox, *op. cit.*) speak is both new and old. In the deepest sense, it continues the reforming spirit of the biblical community of faith. In a more relative sense, it appears new each time the foundations of the religious establishment are shaken by this spirit.

What then is the need for community *per se* in a Christian style of life? What is the essence of communal life? It is social responsibility. It is persons living together in such a way that their decisions are qualified by a concern for the welfare of one another. The essence of communal life is the commitment to submit one's own needs to the needs of others. Even where the underlying motive is self-interest (e.g., self-preservation under the protection of a tribal organization), social responsibility invokes moral values and gives rise to an ethic. Its essence is some *common* value or ideal. The word *community* itself implies this commonality. The sharing of something important forms the basis of community.

If communal life presupposes a common value, the obverse is also true. Because the value has to do with how one relates to other persons, its realization in concrete acts implies a community. This community tries to live according to the value which is its ideal. It also perpetuates the value in time, and may even communicate it to other individuals and communities. In the Bible, where the ultimate value (Love) is personal, and where God takes on personal imagery

(Yahweh in the Old Testament) and a personal mediator (Jesus in the New Testament), this is particularly true. Where faith's object is spirit, as revealed in persons, events, and stories, then faith will be interpersonal. Faith presupposes meaningful interpersonal relationships and their corollary, some community of value. The Church in its essence is a community of common commitment. That the Church in a particular form (e.g., a given congregation in our time) may appear to be far removed from such a community does not alter the definition. If faith is a dynamic response to an ultimate ideal, then the household of faith becomes a community of common commitment. Where a group calls itself the Church and is less than a community of common commitment, it is also less than the Church. Biblically and historically, the community of faith has taken many forms, of which the present parochial/congregational structure of the Church is but one. In pre-exilic times, the form of this community was not distinguishable from the form of the nation-state—for example, under the Davidic monarchy. In post-exilic times and in the period of the New Testament, this community appears as an ethnic group among other ethnic groups, with membership determined primarily by birth. In its early period, before its political establishment by Constantine, the Church was a loose net of underground cell groups with a flexible institutional structure. Before the emergence of religious pluralism in the West, the basic unit of the Church was parochial; a parish designated geographical boundaries rather than a particular socioeconomic unit. And in our time, the form of the Church appears to be congregational (even within those denominations which eschew congregational polity). The Church is focused on a building where a particular group of people (usually defined along socioeconomic lines) gather to engage in "religious" activities under the leadership of individuals designated as religious professionals.

None of the forms of the community of faith then is eternal. Each is culturally and historically relative. Each represents the attempt of the community to order its life in a particular time and place so as to preserve itself and get on with its task. Historically, however, the Church has become ossified in its forms. It has become more concerned with preserving a particular form of its life than with the essential task which forms are intended to facilitate. This is the arteriosclerotic tendency of the religious establishment. When this happens, we have a new idolatry, ecclesiolatry. This is the elevation of a particular form of the community of "called people" to an absolute status, and the consequent worship of the community itself. The central protest of Protestantism was initially against this kind of idolatry. But insofar as Protestantism itself has given rise to a new and increasingly reified religious establishment, the vitality has been sapped from its protest. Indeed, since Vatican II, greater flexibility of form is being demonstrated within Roman Catholicism than within the Protestant establishment.

Ecclesiolatry, like other forms of idolatry, violates the basic biblical understanding of God as spirit, and of "His" relationship to "His" people. To absolutize a particular form of the Church's life, a particular order of ministry (e.g., bishops, priests, and deacons), or particular sacraments so that they become *sine qua nons* of the community of faith is to limit God in time and space. It also inhibits the faith-response of the community of faith. It makes a graven image of the God who is spirit. And it leads to the destruction rather than the perpetuation of the Church. The New Testament word *ekklesia* for this community comes significantly from the verb "to call" (*kaleo*). It designates a group called together. Called together by whom or what? By a particular form of institution which beckons them to join its ranks with the offer of various rewards? No. Called together rather by a spirit which is experienced as a common value. This spirit binds the members of the community together in a way which allows them to nourish one another in their common commitment. At the same time it empowers them to fulfill a common task. The nourishment consists of acts of mutual love which reinforce one another's faith. The "empowering" consists of courage derived from the support of those who share one's commitment. Such courage is necessary where acts of love are not rewarded in kind and where the price of the task can be suffering and death. The task itself is the "mission" of the Church—to love the world in such a way that the world will become more loving itself.

The two classical sacraments of the Church, baptism and holy communion, point to these two functions of its one task. Baptism represents entry into the community, initiation, introduction to the ideal which binds the community together. Thus baptism is symbolic of the goal of the mission—to love the world in such a way that the world responds. Of course, where this is objectified and baptism itself becomes the goal, then the task is trivialized. And the goal of the community becomes little more than ritual acts and increased membership, like any other self-perpetuating social unit.

Likewise, the communion meal represents the mutual nourishment and encouragement of the community. Of course, performance of the ritual does not ensure nourishment. Indeed, petty bickering over the form of the communion often belies or destroys nourishment. Neither does the performance of a baptism ensure genuine entry into the community of faith, or the recitation of marriage vows ensure a genuine marital relationship. Sacraments are rather signs of those intangible qualities and processes which are essential to the life of the Church. Like most signs, they have the power to re-present and make real what they signify. That is, these signs can be mediators. They are not essential to faith in and of themselves. However, it is likely that if discarded some new outward sign would emerge to take their place. Such is the paradoxical nature of a faith which is simultaneously both concrete and abstract. It derives from the life-style of a community which is both spirit-centered and rooted in history.

What has been said of the community of faith here is ideal. It is a description of what the Church can and should be. It is not necessarily a description of what the Church ordinarily is. Some of the factors which inhibit the Church's realization of its essence follow.

INSTITUTIONALIZATION OF THE COMMUNITY

The tendency of the Church to become institutionalized expresses the tendency of all communities to become reified in a particular form. Members of religious communities, particularly as they become further removed from the originating event, fail to distinguish between the essence of their communal life and its particular form. When this happens, communities become subject to the process of institutionalization. Institutionalization is marked by the emergence within the community of a reasonably immutable structure and an increasing concern with the perpetuation of that structure.

It has become fashionable to bemoan the institutionalization of the Church and to yearn romantically after the early pre-Constantinian Church. (Bishop Robinson does this to some extent when he speaks of the Church shearing down some of its institutional superstructure and "travelling light" in our time, *op. cit.*, pp. 25–31.) Such grieving and longing is unrealistic. It fails to recognize that in our technological age, where man understands himself in terms of institutional structures, the Church cannot return to a form derived from rural and agricultural models.[2] More important, such romanticizing forgets that institutionalization itself is inevitable. The process of institutionalization is a two-edged sword. It is as important to the continued life of a community as it is threatening to its integrity. The question for the Church is not whether or not it will become institutionalized, but whether it will recognize its institutionalization and how it will relate to it. Consequently, rather than berate the Church for its institutionalization, we need to call it to an awareness of this process, including its constructive and destructive potential.

The danger of institutionalization lies in the failure to distinguish between spirit and form. For the Church this leads to ecclesiolatry. Likewise, citizens can fail to distinguish between the spirit of their nation and its form at a particular juncture of history. Thus, many Germans failed to see that their national life under the Third Reich violated the spirit of the German people as expressed, for example, in German art, music, and literature. The Nürnberg trials document how misdirected patriotism (devoted to the form and not the spirit of Germany) allowed otherwise sensitive people to support policies which violated their basic values.

Some today feel that American foreign policy is incompatible with the spirit of America as expressed in her art and literature and in the explicit principles on which she was founded (e.g., the right to self-determination). Those who do not distinguish between the form and the spirit of America consider war protesters, for example, unpatriotic. They do not support a particular expression of American life.

In our time American government has become increasingly institutionalized and bureaucratized. There is no turning back the clock on that point, in spite of the tendency of a few rightists to romanticize over lost forms of the American past. However, increasing institutionalization and bureaucratization of government cannot go unheeded by the people whom government is designed to serve, else it will crush their spirit. When government by consensus means that those who criticize (in the name of the communal spirit) are disloyal or unpatriotic, then form is confused with spirit and democracy degenerates into autocracy.

Likewise, the structures of the Church are necessary to function in the modern world. But all structures are transitory and historically relative. They are never absolute. They must be subjected to continuing criticism in the name of the spirit of the Church. This means that no order of the Church's ministry, no ecclesiastical polity, no form of congregational life, no manner of worship, is sacred. As Bishop Robinson puts it, they may all have to "go into the melting pot." [3] How then is the Church to cope with institutionalization, accepting its necessity on the one hand without allowing it to crush its spirit on the other?

Significantly, there is in the biblical faith a resource for this task. It is what Tillich calls "the Protestant principle" [4] (although it is not limited to Protestants). This is the prophetic dimension of biblical faith. It is the reforming spirit of the Judeo-Christian tradition. It is the spirit of self-criticism inherent in biblical faith.

What is this spirit? How is it expressed? And what is its relationship to faith? As one responds to an ultimate value, one measures himself by it. Where the value is seen as spirit, one experiences himself as measured by it. This is what it means to be judged by God. And the judgment is pervasive. It is not limited to personal morality, as is assumed in some forms of American pietism. Instead, this judgment touches all of one's involvements, including the forms by which he lives. Because the individual perceives this judgment and applies the ideal to his own life, the judgment is experienced as self-criticism. For a churchman, self-criticism includes the Church. Hence, he says that the Church stands under the judgment of God. And this is the "Protestant principle," the reforming spirit. It is biblical faith's inherent defense against the dangers of institutionalization.

This principle is most dramatically presented in the prophets of the Old Testament. It is the prophets who call Israel to task for falling short of her ideal, her task in history. It is the prophets who pronounce judgment in the name of the God revealed in the Exodus. It is the prophets who begin their utterances "Thus saith the Lord." And, significantly, it is the prophets who are rejected, cast out as evildoers, and accused of disloyalty to the establishment, even of being unpatriotic.

In the New Testament, there is a prophetic dimension to the

ministry of Jesus. At one level, Jesus was a reformer of the Judaism of his time. He opposed the institutionalism which infected it. Christianity originates as a reformed Judaism. Like most reformers, the first Christians believed their Judaism was the true Judaism. Hence, their reform movement became institutionalized and set over against Judaism.

Luther also embodies this spirit of self-criticism. Recent studies [5] reveal his morbid concern with his failure to live up to the Christian ideal. He subsequently focused the same ruthless conscience on the institutional Church. That Luther finally felt called to identify the Pope as the anti-Christ shows the iconoclastic power of the aroused prophetic spirit. And Luther, like Jesus, never intended to leave the structure he criticized. He saw himself as a part of that structure, a loyal reformer purifying the Church of the idolatries of institutionalization. Like John Wesley, Luther was driven to schism by the intransigency and fear of the agents of the institution he loved and criticized. This is why his critique is as binding on the contemporary Protestant establishment as it is on Roman Catholicism. He was no partisan revolutionary taking pot shots at the establishment from a firm Protestant base. His criticism was self-criticism.

Perhaps the most dramatic prophetic spirit since Luther is Kierkegaard. His denunciation of the religious establishment (in his *Attack Upon Christendom* [6]) still makes uncomfortable reading for even the most radical ecclesiastical critics. Yet Kierkegaard always loved the Church. He never saw himself as detached from her, although he was often alienated. It was only his personal eccentricity (he did not attract any appreciable following until almost a century after his death) which prevented his official separation from the establishment he so mercilessly called to task.

The prophet then stands within the community he criticizes and includes himself in his indictment. This is an important point. Some would-be prophets fail because they remove themselves from the institutionalism which they criticize. Then they no longer know what they are talking about. Or they fail to include themselves under the judgment which they pronounce. The former error leads to irrelevance. The latter leads to self-righteousness. Irrelevance and self-righteousness are dangers inherent in the prophetic mantle. Bertrand Russell, for example, says some very telling things about the Christian Church.[7] But much of what he says is irrelevant because he does not know whereof he speaks "from the inside." Until Russell involves and identifies himself with the Church, his critique remains detached. It runs the risk of setting up a straw man. Likewise, students who storm American embassies abroad to protest foreign policy do not exercise the prophetic voice of American students on this issue. The latter are part of the establishment which they criticize. At their best they include themselves under their own indictment. (And when they lose sight of this, their protest usually goes awry and becomes both irrelevant and self-righteous.) Consequently, they are more "in touch" than foreign students with the system which they criticize, in a better position to have their voice heard (or at least noticed), and usually more realistic in their judgments. In the civil rights movement it is relatively easy to distinguish those who include themselves in their judgments about racism and those who are self-righteous and condemnatory. Both the pronouncements and the activities of the latter are usually irrelevant to the real issues. They justifiably evoke the charge that "they simply don't know what they're talking about." (Illustrative of the way in which involvement tempers the prophet's message with relevance and humility is Reinhold Niebuhr's *Leaves From the Notebook of a Tamed Cynic*.[8] It is an account of his personal responses to people and events during a pastorate in Detroit in the period of the emergence of labor unions.)

Hence, the biblical spirit of self-criticism presupposes involvement in a community of faith. This important resource against institutionalization and ecclesiolatry is "built into" not only the faith-response, but also the faith community. This poses a dilemma for those who stand within the Church but are dissatisfied with her forms. They often find more kindred spirits outside the Church than within her walls. A young clergyman writes: "I find more real Christians among my atheist friends in the peace movement than I see in Church in a month of Sundays!" This leads to a continual temptation to leave the Church, to terminate identification with the idolatry for which she often stands. It is tempting to throw rocks at the stained glass windows from the outside rather than the inside. But one cannot make such a decision without also deciding that the Church itself is lost. It is beyond reprieve or reform, however radical. To say this, one must have found a new communal home or concluded that the communal dimension of faith is an illusion. Increasing numbers of talented, sensitive and honest young men in the ordained ministry have made this decision in recent years. Their number is an index of the Church's institutional dilemma in our time. Others have deep sympathy with such persons, and may one day join their ranks. But not for the present. Some still believe that you can be both a contemporary man and a man of faith,[9] and hold your faith in a community which has some institutional form. This book, particularly this chapter, is an expression of that belief.

PRIESTHOOD AND THE PROBLEM OF AUTHORITY

One mark of the institutionalization of the Church is the emergence of a priestly caste. The development of a priesthood is the religious community's answer to the problem of authority. Even in a democracy (which the Church usually is not), someone must be designated to make decisions on behalf of the people. Someone must *represent* the community in a way that is both authentic and authoritative.

This is the function of the priest. He represents the people. And because he represents the people, they endow him with authority. By establishing a priesthood which is vicarious (i.e., it "stands for" them) the people of the community bind themselves to the policies and doctrines of this priesthood. When priesthood is authentic (i.e., it represents the people) its authority will pose no problems to those who give it or those who hold it. When the priesthood is inauthentic or insufficiently representative, the problem of authority reemerges in a new form. The lack of duly constituted authority is replaced by the authoritarianism of the priesthood. When this threatens the life of the community, the people revolt against the priesthood. But, because the priesthood is identified with the institution, those who revolt usually leave and found a new institution, rather than driving out the priests who have abused their authority.

A second important function of the priestly caste reflects the need for "someone to watch the store." Every institutionalized community requires custodians. They are charged with guardianship of the symbols of the community's life. For the Church this has meant the responsibility and the right to perform ritual acts and to interpret traditions. Priests are ordained (literally: put under orders) to celebrate the sacraments and preach the Word. This custodial function, like the vicarious function of priesthood, carries authority.

The priest determines what is a valid use of the sacraments and what is legitimate preaching of the Word. Here the vicarious and custodial roles of the priesthood coalesce, since the priest exercises his custodial authority in the name of the people. An authentic priesthood wears its authority naturally and "easily." Its use of sacraments and interpretation of Scripture is representative of the life of the community. But an inauthentic priesthood gives rise to authority problems. The sacraments are administered and the Word is preached in ways which violate the integrity of the community. They become inconsistent with the style of the community's life. In popular usage, they are "irrelevant."

The functions of the priestly caste give rise to priestcraft. Priestcraft includes techniques and styles of fulfilling priestly functions. Here too, authority problems emerge. For example, certain ways of celebrating communion become so authoritative that they can be violated only at the risk of desecrating the sacrament itself. This is another form of idolatry. It says that a particular style of worship is absolute and immutable. And it leads to the failure to recognize the sacramental nature of all life. For example, the idolatry of communion can obscure the sacramental potential of every meal. There can be as much communion and thankful self-offering in beer and pretzels at the local bar as in wine and wafers at the local altar.

The emergence of a priestly caste then is both inevitable and dangerous for the community of faith. It is inevitable because communities must solve problems of authority in regard to corporate decision making. It is dangerous because it leads to authoritarianism, the elevation of a caste to a position of veneration. Consequently, there are both advantages and disadvantages to priesthood and priestcraft. This is true even within communities which try to solve the problem by denying the priesthood. The result is a priesthood exercising its authority under cover, without explicit recognition or mandate. This is true, for example, of the executive secretaries of some Quaker meetings, and of many Baptist pastors. The Quaker tradition, which preserves spirit-centered emphases, errs in ignoring the necessity for a concrete medium of the spirit. This leads to an antisacramentalism and anticlericalism which is only an unacknowledged sacramentalism and clericalism.

One advantage of a priestly caste is its visibility. Its functionings can be recognized and challenged when they overstep their mandate.

Another advantage is that *someone* is explicitly charged with a responsibility which cannot be exercised by the community qua community. Even Quakers, with their laudable concept of communal consensus, delegate some authority in the realm of liturgy and program planning to the executive secretary of the meeting. Some meetings even hire a "minister." Likewise, fulfilling both vicarious and custodial functions for a group is an advantage of a recognized priesthood. There is a psychological need for someone who "stands for" the community, for example, in worship. There is a practical and economic need for someone who cares for and preserves the outward signs of the community's life. And there is a theological need for someone who is charged with the responsibility of guarding those outward signs against misuse.

These advantages of a recognized priesthood carry their own dangers. If it is an advantage that the authority of the priest is out in the open where it can be challenged, it is dangerous that this authority is usually spelled out in ritual and document. The priest can appeal to such objective "proofs" to justify an inauthentic priesthood. When ritual and document fall prey to the arteriosclerotic tendencies of organized religion, criticism of priestly authority may be suppressed. This is why, in strong priestly traditions, such as the Roman Catholic and Episcopal Churches, revolts must usually be led by the clergy. Only the priests have the authority to challenge inauthentic authority.

The advantage that some*one* bears responsibilities that cannot be exercised by the whole community carries a corollary danger that the community may abdicate responsibilities that are essentially communal. For example, pastoral care is a responsibility of the entire congregation. But in practice it is often delegated to the ordained clergyman. The consequences for the authenticity of pastoral care can be disastrous. It usually means more to be visited by a concerned friend than by a religious professional who is doing his "duty" and is expected to do "religious" things, like praying.

If it is helpful to focus on one who plays a vicarious role for the community, self-expression can also be stunted when the vicar becomes invested with magical powers. Then he becomes an object of veneration himself. And he inhibits the relationship between the worshipper and his God. Or he becomes so essential that worshipful self-expression cannot take place without him. There is a spurious tradition in this connection with regard to Christian marriage. While the classical understanding has always been that two people marry one another by taking their vows, there is a widespread misconception that the presence of a priest is necessary for the union to be valid. The same is true of baptism in some traditions. Although any believer can baptize another, many churchmen believe that baptism is invalid unless "done" by a clergyman.

The advantage that someone guards the symbols of a community's life carries the danger that he will "possess" those symbols. This removes them from the effective use of the people. The "spooky" way in which the artifacts of the communion service are reserved for the priestly caste (even within Protestantism where we should know better!) is illustrative.

How shall the Church then relate to her priesthood, which appears to be both inevitable and dangerous? There is no better way than applying the "Protestant principle," the spirit of self-criticism. This means that the priesthood is accepted and even welcomed in its inevitability. Indeed, as long as there is a theological rationale for a community of faith, there is also a theological rationale for the priesthood. But the functioning and form of this priesthood must be constantly held up to the critique of the ideal-value, the Spirit. To be effective, this criticism should be practiced by those who belong to the priestly caste as well as by those who do not. That such criticism is presently the sharpest among the clergy is an index of the extent of *hierolatry* [10] in our time. Indeed, in many Protestant circles, the laity strongly resists attempts to dethrone the ordained clergyman from a position of reverence and religious "specialness." To deal with priestly authoritarianism, one must accept responsibility in those areas of ministry traditionally abdicated to the priestly caste. Many laymen appear unwilling to do this. They want their vicar not only to stand for them, but to do for them. Ironically, when the vicar-priest stands for the congregation in unacceptable ways (for example, in publicly expressing his political views), he is often told not to stand for them but simply to "do" religious things for them.

Measuring the priesthood by the Spirit could have radical implications for the form of the Church. In the debate over the criteria of an authentic priesthood, for example, objective variables like "apostolic succession" have confused ecumenical dialogue. Authenticity needs redefinition in more subjective, more spirit-centered, and more meaningful terms. What of the extent to which priesthood represents the faith-response of the community? Therein lies the real priesthood of all believers—a doctrine as often violated within Protestantism as within Roman Catholicism. Likewise, holding the custodial function of priests up to the critique of the Gospel might redefine the guardianship of the sacraments. It could broaden our understanding of desecration. We might see that limiting the communion service to a particular form desecrates its effectiveness as a medium of faith. We might see how misguided guardianship of particular forms practices the very idolatry it seeks to avoid.

Above all, the application of faith's reforming spirit to the priesthood might open our eyes to new forms of priesthood for our time. Just as the parochial structure may be inappropriate today, so the model of the parish ministry may be passé and inappropriate to a truly contemporary priesthood. The day of the paid congregational functionary may be past. His vicarious and custodial functions have accrued so much excess baggage that parish clergy bemoan the demands on their time and often feel ineffective. The community of faith might more effectively fulfill its mission of loving and serving the world if it jettisoned the overburdened priesthood usually identified with the parochial model. Then we might return certain loving and serving responsibilities to the people, where they belong. Some have even proposed a "nonstipendiary" priesthood. This denotes a priestly caste who get paid for doing something besides being priests.[11] Such a priesthood might relieve our clergy of heavy institutional-promotional burdens. And it would highlight their liturgical and custodial functions while de-emphasizing those responsibilities (including even "parish administration") which belong more appropriately to the whole community.

Just as a spirit-centered faith gives rise to a spirit-centered ethic and a spirit-centered community, so a spirit-centered community should give rise to a spirit-centered priesthood. Such a priesthood will be tangible and visible. Some people will continue to be identified and put under orders as priests and others will not. Thus, the ordained priesthood will remain sacramental, an outward and visible sign of the priesthood of the whole community. But a spirit-centered priesthood will be in a constant state of flux regarding its forms. It will be continually holding those forms up to the critique of its God. And insofar as such a priesthood remains loyal to the spirit of the community it serves, it should not be plagued by the kind of authority problems which have haunted the Church.

This doctrine of the priesthood seems consistent with the best intentions of the ecumenical movement, the current reemphasis on the ministry of the laity, and the "worker priest" movements which have emerged since World War II. Perhaps the key to each of these movements is a workable contemporary understanding of that priesthood which is required by a community of faith.

The title "Reverend" is instructive in this regard. It means "worthy of reverence." But one of the problems with today's priesthood is that many revere it for the wrong reasons. They focus on the status of a profession rather than the extent to which one points beyond himself to that which *is* worthy of reverence. This tempts clergy to act "reverent." That means usually to play a role. And "reverent" then comes to means humorless, pretentious, unspontaneous—in short, self-revering. This prompts one alienated student to suggest that what the Church needs is more "irreverent Reverends." Unfortunately, some clergy misinterpret this as a call for a new kind of role playing. It is instead a plea that priests behave like authentic persons by not concealing their humanity.

SOCIAL RESPONSIBILITIES OF THE COMMUNITY

Our earlier discussion of ethics focused on individual decision making. Any morality finally rests on the decisions which individuals make. However, the man of faith is also concerned with *social ethics*. Because the highest value in Christian ethics is the Love defined by Jesus, Christian morality remains indissolubly social. This means more than that the Christian ethic is interpersonal. Christian ethics also have to do with how groups deal with groups. They touch on an individual's responsibility for the attitudes and behavior of any group of which he is a part. Christian ethics are concerned with the very structure of society itself.

The Church today owes a debt to Reinhold Niebuhr for what in its time was a prophetic attack on the "individualistic" ethic of American society and most of American Christianity. In the 20's and the 30's, long before publicity given to the civil rights movement pointed up the immorality of social injustice, Niebuhr was arguing that an ethic which touches only on individual decisions and relationships is insufficient from a Christian perspective. His *Moral Man and Immoral Society* (1936) [12] reminds the individual Christian that he is enmeshed in a social structure for which he is morally responsible. That is the point of social ethics. To speak of a Christian social ethic is to recognize that the Church is morally responsible, not only as the sum of the responsibilities of its individual members, but *qua* community. The Church is a social and political entity which exercises power and is responsible for its use of that power. And the Church is morally responsible not only *as* community. It is also responsible *for* the larger community of which it is a part. The Church is responsible for the moral fiber of the social structure which in part supports it and which it in part supports. No doctrine of the Church, particularly in our time, is complete without acknowledgment of the Church's two-edged responsibility—*as* community and *for* community. It is integral to the Church's style of life.

First then, the Church's responsibilities *as* a community, a social entity: An irony of our time is that a Church that has exercised so much social and political power in the perpetuation of injustice generally refuses to acknowledge this power, let alone exercise it in a way consistent with its love-ethic. It is a truism among modern sociologists and political analysts that the Church is socially conservative, a preserver of the status quo, a bastion against social change. Of course, in isolated instances in the civil rights movement, in the peace movement, and in the present "urban" movement, the Church has been an instrument of social change in our time. On balance, however, the social posture of the Church justifies the harsh judgments passed by most social analysts.

This social conservatism occasionally has a commendable moral basis. Social change is not by definition the work of the Lord, as some reforming zealots suggest. There may be elements of the status quo which situationally require preservation in the name of Love. For example, the de facto racial segregation of some congregations appears contrary to the spirit of the Gospel. But in some situations it can be a means of bringing white people together to confront the real issues of racism before they comfort themselves with token integration. However, preservation of the status quo should be critical and discriminating. The institutional Church must always be open to the possibility that a particular social change is toward a more moral social order. Then it deserves the Church's support rather than its opposition or indifference.

Unfortunately, the characteristic response of the Church in America to social change has been to disavow its political power while supporting practices and structures which need change. This posture often appeals to the principle of the separation of Church and state. In some cases it has made that principle the basis of Christian social ethics. This represents a bad reading of history. The separation of Church and state in the American Constitution does not deny that the Church qua community exercises political power in a democracy. It rather asserts that the Church shall have no structured power over the civil authority and vice versa. The separation of Church and state is designed to protect the ecclesiastical and the civil authorities against the potential authoritarianism of each other.

Of course, this principle has not been wholly successful in protecting the Church against the civil authority in America. This is partly due to the tax-exempt status of the Church. Most denominational bodies and many affluent parishes, for example, hold large investments in the stock market and other aspects of the American economy. But taxwise they qualify as nonprofit institutions. This makes them dependent on the good will of the civil authority. And this becomes an entangling alliance with the political establishment which can compromise the Church's power.

The separation of Church and state then should not be misconstrued as an attempt to disenfranchise the Church. It should not be used to neutralize the political power which the Church can wield as a community of common concern, through the ballot box and through social policies. For example, although it is not imperative that members of a congregation vote as a bloc, increased awareness of common commitment on local political issues (e.g., bussing of schoolchildren, selection of military sites, urban renewal, etc.) could make the Church in a given community a more active political force than it has traditionally been. Or, as has occasionally happened, the Church can itself provide politically controversial or partisan services (such as draft counseling, abortion referrals, and even legal sanctuary) deemed consistent with its mandate.

Such activity presupposes a community of some common commitment. Unfortunately, it is often carried out by an individual clergyman who acts not for the community but only for himself or a minority. Then the Church remains functionally conservative, while an individual uses priestly authority to move in another direction. This usually creates more problems than it solves.

This has been clear in the self-consciousness about race which has marked the American political scene for the past decade. The Church has been one of the institutions which perpetuated racial and other types of discrimination. Pictures of grim-faced vestrymen barring Negroes from worshipping the God of love simply dramatize this. The identification of civil rights with Negro rights (and usually Negro rights in the South) should not allow northern churchmen to become complacent or self-righteous about this expression of the Church's social and political power. Insofar as the residential model of the Church prevails, American Protestant congregations tend to be stratified along socioeconomic lines. These are also usually racial lines. And they are the same lines along which housing and public education are stratified. When this happens, the Church perpetuates the very structure against which much of the civil rights movement has been directed. And individual clerical liberals do not change this exercise of power. They only try to exploit it, usually unsuccessfully.

The same conservative tendency in the exercise of the Church's political power is evident in the emerging peace movement. Almost all American denominations have clergy serving as chaplains in the armed forces. This allegedly serves a pastoral function, ministering to the needs of young churchmen separated from their home congregations by the necessities of military service. But the presence of chaplains also gives the tacit approval of the religious establishment to the work of the military establishment. More explicitly, chaplains intone benedictions of the God of love on young men embarking to wreak destruction and death on another people. And clergymen ascend their pulpits to reassure their people that the killing being done in their name is justified and endorsed by the spirit of the Christian Gospel. Anyone who observes this service of the religious establishment to the civil authority and continues to believe that the Church exercises no political power is either blind or intransigent.

The Church does exercise power as a community. Indeed, in its own self-understanding, we have seen that the Church *is* power. It is dynamic because it is a community of those whose style of life is dynamic. The moral question then is not whether or not the Church should exercise social and political power, but how it exercises that power. The answers to that question will determine the social responsibilities of the community of faith at a given time and place.

These illustrations do not imply that the Church must always be *for* civil rights and *against* war. The new morality applies to social as well as individual ethics. The Church as a community must determine its moral posture on a given issue in a given context. This will probably vary locally, from one congregation to the next. And certainly variation is to be expected on social and political issues within a congregation. The imperative of a Christian social ethic is simply that the Church as community take seriously its responsibilities on such issues, rather than pretend its power does not exist.

But if it takes its social responsibilities seriously, the Church must make sometimes agonizing decisions on the burning issues of the day. And then it must put those decisions into action in the form of its own life as well as in its public posture. To refuse to make decisions concerning the responsible exercise of political power is to decide not to decide. That usually means to go along with the subtle exercise of ecclesiastical power which characterizes the status quo. Although it is not always true that "silence gives consent," it has been generally true of the Church vis-à-vis social injustice in our time.

Social responsibility *as* a community then means self-consciousness about the implications of a love-ethic on issues like education, taxation, community spending, slum clearance, selective service, etc. And it then means acting as a community, where possible, on this self-consciousness. Where it is impossible for the Church to act as a community (for example, because of the nature of the issue or for lack of a clear consensus), then this self-consciousness can still stimulate individual social action.

The Church's responsibilities *as* a community imply responsibilities *for* the larger community (town, city, state, nation-state). Indeed, these two dimensions of social ethics are so inseparable that it is impossible to discuss one without the other. The ways in which the Church exercises its political power reflect its attitude toward the social order. Because the Church is dependent on the social order, it is also responsible for the moral fiber of that order. And moral fiber does not mean simply the "morals" of the individuals who make up the social order—the extent to which they cheat, steal, sleep with each other's wives, fudge on their income taxes, park illegally, and in other ways transgress the law. The moral fiber of a social order has to do also with its structure and the ways in which it encourages or inhibits the full humanity of its members. The moral fiber of a particular social order, from a Christian perspective, has to do with the extent to which its structure is consistent with the love-ideal of the Gospel.

Herein lies the relationship between love and justice.[13] As long as man exists in a world of social relationships and responsibilities, Christians cannot speak of the love of the Gospel in a purely individualistic frame of reference. You cannot speak of love without speaking also of justice. Justice is the social expression of love. Justice is love actualized in the social order, not simply in individual self-giving.

Some prefer to keep love in the realm of religion and individual relationships, and justice in the realm of politics and corporate relationships. But this cannot be done within a Christian faith-response. Not only is Jesus' own ministry an eminently social ministry to the poor, the needy, the disinherited, and the rejected.[14] But there is also something incongruous about a middle-class American practicing love in his personal relationships while not acting to correct the injustices of a social order which deprives large numbers of people of the benefits of middle-class life. He too easily forgets that those benefits define the context in which he loves.

The man whose God is defined by the Cross can ignore the relationship between love and justice only at his peril. His particular Cross may be the loss of some of his cherished comforts in the name of a more just and loving social order.

Those who object that no social order can make people love one another are right. But they are only half right. They forget that a more just social order can provide a context in which their highly individualistic love-ethic can flourish in a more universal way. The present racial and class hatred on the American scene cannot be alleviated simply through individual acts of kindness, however altruistic. These hatreds and suspicions are too deeply grounded in the realities of social injustice. They will only be alleviated when the context in which races and classes attempt to live together has been reformed. Such a social reformation in the direction of a more love-capable and just social order is a burning issue confronting the Church in our time. Will it help to speed reformation? Or will it inhibit it? And how will it exercise its responsibility for the social order? As the sum of the efforts of individual Christians? Or in some collective action *qua* Church?

Some will ask at this point for specific guidelines as to how the Church can act *as* a community *for* the larger community. There are no easy answers to that question. Perhaps the answer lies in another question: How can the Church *be* as a community? How can individual Christians be in community without becoming indistinguishable from other communities—like the country club, the Rotary, or the Elks? How can this communal dimension of a Christian style of life be expressed in our time?

On the answers to those questions hangs the judgment which future generations will pass on the Church in twentieth-century America. In such a crisis, it has become popular for Christians to speak of the need to "christianize" the nation, to christianize the city, or to christianize one's own community. In the broadest meaning of "christianize," this is appropriate. The task of the Church *is* so to love the world (the nation, the city, the community) that it itself becomes more loving. But the christianizing of a community has come to mean endowing it with the symbols and outward signs of Christian life. Thus, the christianization of the nation might mean the election of more "Christians" to public offices; the christianization of the city might mean more churches in the inner city, where underfed black children can be photographed carrying a cross through the streets; the christianization of one's community might mean more people going to church, and more pleas on radio and television to "patronize" the church of your choice. Where christianization degenerates into preoccupation with contentless symbols, sensitive Christians should stop talking about christianizing the nation or any social unit. Real christianization will not be recognizable by such trivial outward signs. It will be marked instead by the moral integrity of the nation-state and the social order and policies which it perpetuates.

Our task as Christians then may be simply to call upon the nation to be more fully what it can be, should be, and claims to be. Our task is to call upon the nation *really* to be a community of justice and equality for all, and to use every legitimate instrument of political power at our disposal in this call.[15] That is the essence of the social responsibility of the Church in our time.

It is usually easier to talk about what the Church ought to be than about what it is. But this leads to irrelevant romanticizing about an ideal Church and moral self-flagellation, to the neglect of coming to grips with the compromised posture of the Church. It can also lead to the dangerous illusion that the Church is what it ought to be, that the Church actually is what it is ideally. (Cox implies this at times, as, for example, when he speaks of the Church as God's *avant-garde* with insufficient acknowledgment of how very rarely the Church in our time is in any serious way theologically or socially *avant-garde*.)

At the same time, to speak only of what the Church is, is to offer a purely sociological analysis. It also simply adds to the growing literature which excoriates the Church for her moral hypocrisy in social ethics. This literature should be taken more seriously than it has been by churchmen. But we also need a literature which explores the possibility and promise of a meaningful faith and viable style of life for the Church. That is the intention of the present volume.

A VISIBLE AND AN INVISIBLE CHURCH

Apparently, then, the true Church is not always the community which calls itself the Church. The spirit of the community of faith is not always coterminous with the form of the institutional Church.

This insight has led to the classical distinction between a visible and an invisible Church.[16] Although rejected by some as too "mystical"[17] and by others as question-begging,[18] the distinction is helpful in dealing with the ambiguities of the Church as it is. It is also necessary for a spirit-centered theology based on a distinction between spirit and form.

In addition, to speak of a visible and an invisible Church is to acknowledge not only that the institutional Church does not fulfill her task, but also that other communities do fulfill it. This includes in faith's community those who appear to be living their lives in response to the same spirit without using the religious labels. The concept of an invisible Church allows the man of faith, for example, to make sense out of the loving actions of atheists in the civil rights movement when compared with the behavior of pious churchgoers who have opposed them. It allows one to see the love of God operative in the new peace movement while the Church generally assumes an antipacifist posture. Of course, to recognize one's God among those who do not use one's labels does not make them into unconscious or naïve believers. That may be the way a believer sees it, but it is not necessarily the way the nonbeliever sees it.

To speak of an invisible Church then is not to ascribe some concealed form of Christianity to those who do not espouse it. It simply recognizes a kindred spirit. It recognizes the important functional community which binds men together when they serve a common cause. Such a recognition is inevitable if one has a clear perception of the spirit he is serving.

A schematic presentation illustrates this distinction. Imagine two large circles which overlap one another only slightly so that by far the largest part of each circle is not included in the other. Call one circle the invisible Church and include all whose lives are lived in response to the spirit which is the love of Christ. Call the other circle the visible Church. It includes all those who identify themselves as Christians and "belong" to the institutional Church.

The relevance of the symbol for our time is revealed in the relative size of the three areas included in the two circles. On the one hand, there are many people whose life-style actualizes the spirit of the Gospel, but who do not identify themselves as Christians. On the other hand, there is an equally significant number of individuals who identify themselves as Christians but who do not appear to be responding to the spirit of the Gospel. Then in the middle there is that small group belonging to both communities. They both behave like and call themselves Christians. They practice what they preach, and conversely preach what they practice. And, of course, beyond the two circles there is a larger community of those who neither call themselves Christians nor appear to respond to the Love/spirit.

A PERSONAL NOTE

This chapter on the Church must close on a personal note. A central vocational tension for many younger clergy in recent years has been a growing dissatisfaction with the institutional Church. The problem is no longer simply that the Church fails to live up to her ideal. It is a live option that the Church in our time may be of all institutions the most incorrigibly opposed to its own ideal.

One sees this in the preoccupation with self-interest which infects the principalities and powers of the Church. A bishop of the Episcopal Church, for example, has written me that his decision in an important matter was governed by his estimate of "what is best for the Diocese." But what happens when "what is best for the Diocese" runs contrary to the spirit of Christ?

One sees the same tendency in the "edifice complex" which defines clerical success and congregational mission in terms of building programs. In most denominational magazines one can find an article depicting the "success" of an energetic, usually young, clergyman, who has "built up" his congregation to the point of encumbering it with a lovely new parish house. One may even see a bishop or other ecclesiastical authority blessing this edifice with a crucifix, the symbol of self-emptying love.

One sees this problem also in the infectious self-promotion which makes clergy and laity alike more concerned with the number of sheep in the corral on a given Sunday morning than with the quality of the pabulum they are usually fed. As one colleague, serving a lightly attended rural mission, wisely puts it: "The good Lord told us to feed the sheep, not to count them."

A similar principle is evident every time a decision by an important governing council of the Church is dictated by self-preservation. Unfortunately, even some of the current ecumenical ferment has such a basis. It is a kind of fearful uniting of Christians against a common enemy—the world—which appears to be threatening the Church's very foundations with its processes of secularization. This, of course, is not true of all ecumenical efforts. Much ecumenical concern is functionally oriented, and represents not retreat, but an advance to serve the world.

Even the moral hypocrisy of academic and commercial institutions often does not appear as blatantly anti-Christ as the functionings of the institutional Church in our time.[19]

Those are harsh words. In some circumstances, they would be unfair words. But on balance they describe the Church as it appears to many within. They are an index of the tension some of us experience between convictions concerning a community of faith and the form of the community as we know it. Our posture toward the Church becomes then one of loyal opposition. Sometimes this opposition becomes so radical that it appears disloyal. I cannot myself see such opposition as disloyal as long as I entertain any possibility that the Church can become more fully what it ought to be and ideally is. But as long as it is also a live option that the Church is the agency of that spirit which is anti-Christ, propounding all of the idolatries which inhibit man's response to the biblical God and opposing the historical actualization of the love of Christ, then my opposition is also potentially disloyal.

Perhaps the hardest task for the man of faith in our time is to live with these tensions and all of their possibilities. That too is part of the style of life called faith. It is part of being in community.

5

doing religious things

THE PREVIOUS CHAPTER touched only peripherally on the formal activities of the religious establishment. These are the "religious" practices: worship, prayer, and other formal expressions of religious discipline.

A recurrent question in this time of theological revolution is: what about prayer and worship? This is particularly true in the popular response to the "death of God" theologies and other rejections of God as a discrete being. A spirit-centered theology also evokes such questions. Unfortunately, they have been avoided by the majority of the radical theologians of the new era.[1] This is because most of the "new" theologies have little to say concerning what has traditionally been identified as prayer and worship. Their starting point, a frontal assault on the existence of God, appears to remove the linchpin from most traditional religious practices.

From a spirit-centered perspective, however, this need not be so. Doing religious things can remain meaningful without the existence of a supreme being. Our understanding of appropriate forms of prayer and worship, however, may need to be radically altered. A spirit-centered theology distinguishes the spirit of prayer and worship from the forms which need to go into the melting pot in the twentieth century. That is the intention of the present chapter.

What is the difference between prayer and worship? Where does one end and the other begin? A clear-cut distinction is impossible.

116

But, in general, worship refers to the corporate dimension of that activity of which prayer is the individual dimension. Thus, it is only proper to speak of prayer/worship, although it is helpful to distinguish between the two as different forms of a similar process. Acknowledging that there is a prayerful dimension to all worship and a worshipful dimension to all prayer, worship should be examined first. It is the ground of prayer in the same way that life in community is the ground of a meaningful individual life-style.

WORSHIP IN THE NEW ERA

A proper understanding of worship lies in the English roots of the word: worth-ship. To worship is to ascribe worth. It is to express and demonstrate that which is worthwhile (literally: worth one's time). It is to show what is important in one's life and in the life of the worshipping community. Where worship refers to self-conscious religious practices, it means "rendering worth" to that which is ultimately important for a community.[2]

Worship then expresses man's faith-response, particularly in its communal form. Worship is the community of faith *offering* itself to and for the spirit it calls ultimate. The dimension of offering is crucial because the most complete way to show what is really important is to give oneself to and for it. Above all the words, above all the outward and visible gifts which may represent our self-giving, the most valuable "thing" that each of us has to give is his own self. Thus, a man for whom the spirit of his country represents the ultimate value may give his life for his country. (The patriotic fervor evoked by Nathan Hale's "I only regret that I have but one life to lose for my country" reflects the ultimate nature of the statement.) A man for whom money is the ultimate value may literally give his life to the accumulation of money (and we say colloquially that he "worships money"). A man for whom the love of Christ is the ultimate value will give his life for this cause. Such giving of one's life does not necessarily mean giving up one's life (dying), although on occasion it may in the literal, physiological sense. It does mean, however, submerging one's own interests to the cause of the spirit which one worships. When a community says this in its worship, it makes its own self-interest secondary to the service of its God-spirit. This means that on occasion the Church may be called to give up its own life (literally to die!) in order to serve the cause of Him whom the Church calls Lord.

This understanding of Christian worship should frighten anyone who worships. It probably would frighten most churchgoers out of such a radical practice if they understood what they were saying. This is one reason the moral hypocrisies of the institutional Church are so perplexing and frustrating to those who serve her professionally. They are inconsistent with her worship as self-offering.

Of course, worship as self-offering is not limited to what goes on at a particular time and place on Sunday morning. Worship is much broader and comprehends every activity in which a community expresses its ultimate value. However, the word is generally used only to designate particular, periodically recurring occasions. It is the formal activities of these occasions that those who ask, "What about worship in the new era?" usually have in mind. This activity might be called "formal worship."

Because such an activity is formal, it should be no less self-sacrificing. However, the loss of self-offering is precisely what often happens to formal worship. An inverse proportion between the form and the essence of worship develops. As the form increases the essence (genuine self-offering) appears to decrease. This is not a necessary development, as some Puritan reformers assume. (The Puritan intention vis-à-vis worship is to "purify" it of the formalism which is always potentially idolatrous. This leads to a certain dryness and lack of color in much Puritan worship, and eventually leads to a formalism of formlessness.) However, the word *formal* does point to a key problem for worship. This is to develop a form appropriate to the self-offering of a particular community at a particular time and place, which does not itself become an object of worship. Hence, the problem of worship could be solved by a form which has within itself the principle and the means of its own self-destruction. We shall return to this suggestion subsequently.

A corollary of worship's problem of form is the problem of language.[3] Actually, the two are inseparable since the language people use when worshipping is a form of self-expression. Language is particularly a problem in our time when the words of most Protestant worship continue to reflect the milieu of the sixteenth-century Reformers. Even where language has been "updated," one usually finds only a translation of sixteenth-century vocabulary into the vernacular rather than the wholesale substitution of a new vocabulary. How then resolve this two-pronged problem of the form and language of worship for modern man?

We need to begin with the marks of Christian worship in our time. They are: (1) a community of religiously like-minded people gathered (2) in a building designated as a house of worship, (3) at a time and day of the week which has some religious significance, and (4) engaged in directing prayers, hymns, creeds, their attention, and other more tangible gifts toward their God or his designated representative. In the Judeo-Christian tradition a basic form for such activities is a common meal. However, this has been so distorted by sacramentalists and antisacramentalists alike as to be almost unrecognizable in much Christian worship today. (Sacramentalists tend to convert the communion service into a magical rite, and hence obscure the dimension of self-offering through a common meal. Antisacramentalists are so anxious to avoid this error that they neglect the dimension of a common meal in their worship—e.g., the preoccupation of Low Church Episcopalians with Morning Prayer to the relative neglect of the common meal.)

The questions for today's man of faith are: Do these traditional criteria exhaust worship for him? And, do these practices give authentic expression to his self-offering?

To the first question, a spirit-centered theology must answer: No. Worship as self-offering cannot be contained within any particular form. To the second question, the man who perceives his God as spirit will give a qualified Yes and No. Particular forms may or may not be expressive for him or his community. It depends, among other things, on the extent to which he is able to recognize the spirit behind the forms and the extent to which they reflect something that really goes on in his life.

To say No to the first question is to be genuinely open-ended in regard to the form of one's worship. It is to recognize that any corporate activity can become formal worship. Thus, the singing of freedom songs at a civil rights meeting does not need to be baptized with Christian prayers or religious language to be authentic worship of the Christian God ("who" is a spirit of freedom from bondage!). Likewise, the *joie de vivre* of spring vacation on the beaches of Fort Lauderdale does not need a religious professional who distributes wafers and wine to be genuine self-offering to the biblical spirit.

To give a qualified Yes and No to the second question asserts the relativity of all forms of worship. One need be neither uncritically antagonistic to nor accepting of the forms of worship passed down through the traditions of the Church. I must ask, for example, of the traditional communion service: What am I saying here about myself and my life? Am I saying anything meaningful and real to me? Are there other forms through which I (we) might say the same thing more effectively and more meaningfully? Most importantly, does this form of worship really ascribe worth to *my* God?

To assert the relativity of the forms of worship is to be a continuous liturgical reformer. It is to be constantly asking whether yesterday's form expresses today's commitment. That we have a liturgical movement in our time bent on such reform is from one perspective commendable. From another, it is shameful that the Church is not in a constant state of liturgical movement.

The form of worship should be continually subject to the same self-critical principle which applies to the Church's ministry and institutionalization. Therefore, one dimension of life offered up in worship is the form of worship itself. That calls for scrupulous honesty in worship. We have seen that Christian faith calls for critical demolition as a prelude to healthy reconstruction.

It is the problem of language, however, which is foremost for those who try to reconcile a spirit/God with the deity of traditional worship language. The latter lives in a place called heaven, hears prayers, sees what goes on in the world, and intervenes in the processes of nature and the course of history, sometimes at His own whim and sometimes in response to requests. The language of traditional worship is, of course, derived from the biblical tradition with its associated view of the world. But biblical language reflects a world view which is foreign to twentieth-century man. To superimpose this language on his worship is to violate the subjectivity of faith. It also makes faith appear quaint and antiquated, concerned primarily with preserving customs of only historical interest. To impose biblical language on the modern man who is already having intellectual difficulties with a God who exists may prevent him from expressing a genuine faith-response within the Church.

What then are we to do with this "outdated" language which continues to speak of God as if he were a man who lives in the sky, when the vast majority of even theologically conservative churchmen have ceased to believe in such a deity? There are at least three steps to a viable approach.

First, we should recognize that all theological language, and especially the language of the Bible, is more akin to the language of poetry and imagination [4] than to the language of the laboratory and of quantification. Theological language, like poetry, is designed to express the reality of the spirit. Biblical language is metaphorical before it is metaphysical. It makes verbal pictures out of real-life experiences and then uses them to communicate its spirit. To objectify this language is as absurd as to objectify the grade-school illustration of metaphor: "The moon was a ghostly galleon tossed upon cloudy seas." [5] Actually, this first step of de-objectifying worship language has been made (sometimes unconsciously) by many modern churchmen. There are few Episcopalians, for example, who believe that God possesses a humanlike hand, although the *Book of Common Prayer* continues to speak of God in this way.

But the recognition of worship language for what it is may not be enough. The metaphors themselves may be inappropriate to the real-life experiences of people in the context of twentieth-century society. The image of a redeemer, for example, was more expressive in a social milieu where people were regularly purchased out of bondage (redeemed) for a price than it is today. The metaphor of the shepherd evokes an experience which is foreign to increasing numbers of contemporary men. A second task of the language strategy of our time, then, must be a searching of the metaphors and images delivered to us for their meaning *in their time*. In other words—to what dimension of faith's experience do the redeemer and shepherd images point? This is a step which has also been taken by some contemporary churchmen. However, not everyone can be a Semitic scholar and steep himself in the milieu which produced our biblical symbols and images. Hence, still more is required.

The third step must be the searching out of new images to express the meaning of faith for us here and now. We simply cannot continue genuinely to offer ourselves to a God who is identified in terms foreign to our experience. That leads to magic or superstition, or both. We need twentieth-century metaphors. These will be as relative and conditioned as the first-century metaphors to which we still cling. But they will be drawn from the world in which we live and move and have *our* being. They will be borrowed from the realms of technology, business, political action, rapid transportation, psychedelics, outer space—in short, from all those realms which shape the contemporary vocabulary.

For example, what are the analogies between congregational worship and a sit-in? What child of today does not have all kinds of concrete associations with a phrase like "A-OK"? We have been very traditional in this book in referring to Jesus as a mediator. From the modern realms of electronics or labor relations, one might evoke the image of a conductor or a go-between. In business, this is the role of the middleman. He makes the connections between otherwise unconnectable parties.

The psychedelic vocabulary, which has already made a discernible impact on advertising, could inform faith's vocabulary. To be "turned on," "tuned in," "in touch," "flying high," "spaced," refer to real experiences. These are analogous, if not identical, to faith's experience. As we begin to recognize the religious dimensions of some drug usage, perhaps we can also begin to express our worship in a more vital and contemporary language. There are already signs of this in such experiments as "The Electric Mass."

Likewise, the rhetoric of the New Left and the present black movement is relevant to religious expression. When some speak of the "Establishment" or the "System," especially in monolithic and conspiratorial terms, they are confessing an experience analogous to "principalities and powers" in the Pauline literature.[6] When black people speak of their need to "get ourselves together," they are referring to a basic experience of a community of common history and commitment.

In short, we must constantly strive to keep our worship in a real vernacular, a language understood by the people. And the language of traditional worship is often simply dead because its referents are dead.

Such a linguistic strategy sets the stage for new forms for worship. From a Christian perspective, an important principle here will be self-criticism and potential self-destruction. Where one respects the relativity of all forms, it is presumptuous to prescribe new forms as if they were *the* forms for our time. That task probably belongs to units at least as small as individual congregations. It would provide a fruitful exercise in honesty and self-examination for any congregation courageous and free enough to undertake it. However, in a classical understanding of worship there are clues to the general directions new forms of worship might take.

One clue is the relationship between worship and a man's work, that primary "occupation" to which he gives himself. Work here does not mean simply a man's job—whether, for example, he is a plumber or a garbage collector or a student or a priest. It means this, but it means much more. A man's work is that activity to which he gives himself. Sometimes it does not include his job, which is irrelevant to his real work. More often it has some relationship to his job. It is with such an understanding of work, for example, that people call themselves civil rights "workers," even though they are also engaged as students, sharecroppers, teachers, doctors, etc. A man's work is one way he expresses his worship. In terms of time alone, it is one of the most pervasive modes of self-offering. The Church has always understood that there is an integral relationship between work and worship. The technical word for a form of worship, *liturgy,* means "the work of the people." [7]

What does this relationship imply for new forms of worship? Primarily, that they should have something to do with what a man does with his time. This means that worship should be more functionally oriented. The forms of worship themselves can be derived from the functions men fulfill in the service of their God. The spirit of the Gospel (identified biblically as the Truth [8]), for example, can be worshipped in a classroom in which truth is genuinely pursued. And the methods of the classroom can influence the form of our worship. Worship in our time, like good education in our time, needs to be more dialogue than monologue. Likewise, the worship of the biblical God might be recognized in the ritualized form of some militant political meetings. Conversely, the spirited controversy of political meetings in hammering out strategies for a common cause might bring new life to the Church's formal worship.

Would such new forms of worship include the principle of self-criticism? As long as we remain functional in our orientation, it would appear so, since functions change. This is presently clear in civil rights groups which are experiencing a tension between forms of action appropriate to 1956 and those which are appropriate today. Just as the Church can appear to be the Society for the Preservation of Wafers and Wine, so, without the flexibility of a functional orientation, the civil rights movement could become the Society for the Preservation of Massive Marches.

At the same time, a functional orientation uncovers new communities of worship, defined along other than denominational lines. This also should introduce a spirit of self-criticism since most functionally oriented communities are called to die. They should die either in the process of fulfilling their function or *ex post facto.*

All of this points to the need for a broader definition of worship. Like the broader understandings of faith, ethics, the Church, and ministry which a spirit-centered theology suggests, this view of worship need not be antagonistic to the forms delivered to us. It is antagonistic only to worship which limits faith's self-offering to certain forms. It is antagonistic only to that which inhibits meaningful expression of one's style of life.

PRAYER IN THE NEW ERA

Prayer is an individual expression of worship. It is usually a more personal, less formalized, highly individual activity through which one offers himself. Prayer thus defined is what some call "private prayer."

To recognize private prayer as grounded in worship acknowledges its dimension of self-offering. Indeed, prayer should be viewed under the heading of self-offering, although many discussions ignore this dimension. Then prayer is reduced to conversations with a hypothetical supreme being.[9]

To view prayer as self-offering sheds light on the classical forms of prayer, and vice versa. These are: Adoration, Confession, Petition, Intercession, and Thanksgiving. Each is a form of self-offering.

A prayer of adoration is essentially the offering up of one's awe before the object of one's faith. When God is understood as spirit, one is saying to this spirit: "You" are the most important reality in my life. I stand in awe before "your" power, as it has been demonstrated in my life. I adore "You" and offer myself in "your" service. This is self-offering.

Likewise, the prayer of confession represents the offering of oneself in all of one's frailty as measured by the Spirit. A prayer of confession says in effect: In spite of these specific instances when I have failed to live up to the ideal which "You" are, I offer myself to "your" service. I do this with no illusions concerning my future behavior, but in the confidence that strengthened by my commitment to "You," I can always make a new start; Love is an ever-new responsibility and possibility. Thus understood, the prayer of confession presupposes penitence (measuring oneself against the ideal-value), absolution (the washing away of past failures), and rededication (the determination to "do better").

Petition too is best understood as self-offering. In prayers of petition the pray-er offers to his God himself, including all of his most passionate desires and needs. The inclusion of prayers of petition in the Christian tradition shows an awareness that self-offering is total. One does not hold back anything, not even desires and needs which seem unacceptable. Of course, if the self-offering is total, such prayers are given with the understanding "nevertheless not my will but thine be done." [10] Desires and needs are expressed by one who knows that they should not be fulfilled if they are contrary to the cause of the Spirit. Petition as self-offering does *not* assume that God acts in some magical and independent way to fulfill one's needs. It means only that the needs themselves are a dimension of my self-offering. The action may indeed finally come from myself.

The danger of pseudomagical manipulation of the deity is even more apparent in the prayer of intercession. Here, one specifically asks for something, for someone or some cause for which one is concerned. Prayers of intercession provide a great stumbling block for twentieth-century man because they imply a separate being who intervenes in the course of events on request. Yet here again a view of prayer as self-offering is revealing. The real meaning of intercession is the offering up of one's intention and concerns for others. Properly understood, these are not offered up in the belief that some magical superman will take care of them, but rather with the understanding that intentions, concerns and desires for others are an inextricable part of us. One cannot offer himself without also offering such intentions. Indeed, in the process of offering up intentions they may be refined in the light of the Spirit. This will be reflected in one's style of life.

Some have tried to resolve the cause-and-effect dilemma of intercessory prayer by praying only for those with whom they have some direct contact. Intercessory prayer is then limited to situations where one can translate it into action. Though commendable in spirit, this solution misses the point of prayer as self-offering. It is appropriate today, for example, to pray for the people of Vietnam, even if one will probably never see them and may have only the most indirect influence on their welfare. It is appropriate because one is concerned for the people of Vietnam. The validity of such an offering depends on the genuineness of the intention and its compatibility with one's ultimate commitments, not on the possibility of translating intentions into results. It is assumed that one will take every opportunity to translate intercessions into actions. That is one mark of their genuineness. Significantly, prayer may even serve to heighten self-consciousness in this area.

The prayer of thanksgiving is also a form of self-offering. It is an explicit offering up of gratitude for what one has experienced of his God. It says that because of what the Spirit has given me I give myself in response to the cause of the Spirit. In biblical terms, we love because He first loved us.[11] Many prayers of thanksgiving obscure this by focusing on the tangible, material comforts of human existence. Of course, each of us should be grateful for such comforts. But to make them the focus of thanksgiving is to make God into a divine sugar daddy. It also misses the point that the focal gift is the gift of the Spirit itself. In traditional terms, this is God's self-giving, or self-emptying. For the Christian, the basic gratitude is because *for him* the spirit of Love has been demonstrated and made real in the personage of Jesus. Therefore, a Christian style of life involves living thankfully.

To view prayer as self-offering, however, still begs the central prayer question of our time: "But who in the world am I praying to?"

That is a serious question when God has been deobjectified. And it is an important question for a spirit-centered theology which challenges the existence of God on theological grounds. Other "radical" theologies have usually either ignored this question or dealt with it inadequately. Even Bishop Robinson's treatment,[12] which suggests that one's whole life is a prayer, is insufficient. It is true that one can and should view his whole life as a prayer. But that does not really solve the riddle: Who is the other party? Or, is there no other party?

For a spirit-centered theology, it is only metaphorically appropriate to speak of "another party" to prayer. The question "Who in the world am I praying to?" posits an object of faith and prayer "who" is a person with discrete being in time and space. But spirit-centered faith rejects such an understanding of God. Is that then all there is to say on the subject? Is prayer simply part of the excess baggage which must be jettisoned by the modern man of faith? No. Even the most traditional forms of prayer can be expressive of a spirit-centered theology.

How? The other "party" in prayer is indissolubly spirit. Therefore, one is offering oneself (albeit usually in verbal address) to a spirit. But in the Christian tradition this spirit is neither amorphous nor impersonal. It is identified through a person, Jesus of Nazareth. Hence, Jesus becomes a mediator of prayer, and formal Christian prayers end with the ascription "through Jesus Christ our Lord." This is a metaphor. It does not mean that Jesus is an objective person presently existing somewhere within time and space. He is not a kind of Gemini control through whom messages must be checked or relayed in order to reach the real source of power. The metaphor of Jesus as mediator means something which is both more real and more subjective. It means that one offers himself to his God through imagining that Spirit in its primal experiential form. Only with such a view can we avoid misunderstanding in calling prayer a form of communication. The pray-er *is* expressing himself verbally, as in normal discourse, because the object of his faith "appears" to him in a personal form. This personal form is defined in such a way that you cannot carry on a simply self-contained conversation where you are both parties. Because the medium of faith is concrete (i.e., he is portrayed in the New Testament as a certain kind of person), the pray-er cannot put words in the mouth of the other "party." To this extent, and *only to this extent,* can God be said to take the initiative in prayer—according to a spirit-centered understanding.

An illustration from personal experience may clarify this point. When I am concerned about something, I often find myself inadvertently in an imaginary conversation. This usually happens as I lie in bed waiting for sleep to overtake me. But it is not limited to such occasions and sometimes happens in the hustle of my daily routine. The people with whom I carry on such "conversations of imagination" are limited in number. They are those who have been unusually significant in my life, mediators of the Spirit which calls forth my "style." As a Christian, this means mediators of the Christ-spirit to me, persons who have been Christ to me. These conversations are very real and often very helpful. They not only force me to clarify my own values in a given situation. They also bring to bear the commitment or the spirit of another. Because that "other" is a concrete person with identifiable traits and values (e.g., it is frequently a parent or certain teachers), there is no possibility of putting words in his mouth. The personal image, built on my experience, will not tolerate it. Indeed, the "other" is often critical of what I am doing or thinking. He holds my self-offering up to the light of the Spirit which we both acknowledge. I believe that such conversations are the very essence of prayer, and provide insight into its internal dynamics. I am in effect offering myself in terms of certain concrete decisions to the spirit which I call God. And I am doing it through conversation with concrete mediators of that Spirit.

This illustration points up the validity of prayer through the saints. In recognizing the idolatry to which a succession of historical mediators can lead, Protestantism has generally rejected this psychologically sound practice. If a saint is an historical personage who gives form to the spirit of the Gospel (discounting the pseudo-objective procedures by which sainthood is determined), then prayer through the saints reflects the type of conversation just cited.

It is often said that prayer is autosuggestion. Insofar as this is reductionistic (i.e., prayer is *nothing but* autosuggestion and therefore inherently illusory), it does not come to grips with the complicated data of prayer. But, the reductionistic bias notwithstanding, the observation itself is sound. Prayer *is* autosuggestion, where the dialogue takes place within the imagination of one individual. Out of the data of his experience he suggests the content of prayer *on both sides*. Only one who fears the subjectivity of faith and clings to the idolatry of an existing God will refuse to acknowledge this.

Prayer then is not passé in an era when the God of traditional metaphysics is either dead or gasping. A spirit-centered theology which proclaims the death of that God reaffirms the integrity of prayer as an expression of faith. However, it does not necessarily reaffirm all of the traditional language of prayer. Some of that may have to go into the melting pot with the existing God of whom it speaks. Out of this melting should come a broadened definition of prayer. It will be based on the understanding that the essence of prayer is self-offering. It should include Bishop Robinson's insight that all of one's life is a prayer. And it should also include "conversations of imagination."

With a broadened definition, a spirit-centered theology will continue to call for honesty in and about our prayer life. Honesty *in* prayer means saying what one means and meaning what one says. This conflicts with the use of alien forms and language simply because they seem more "religious." Honesty *about* prayer means describing our prayer life in terms of what it really is, rather than in terms of what we think it ought to be. A failure to be honest *about* prayer plagues many popular manuals on this subject, as well as some well-intentioned prayer groups.

Another personal illustration points this up. In my first year in seminary, every entering student took a course in the meaning and practice of prayer. The appropriate manuals were prescribed and read, and animated discussions often ensued. Some beautiful and, no doubt, true things were said about prayer in those discussions. However, many of us felt that the discussions and the reading did not really touch anything authentic in our own experience. And the conviction grew in us that we had no real prayer life. I suspect that many who have participated in prayer-discussion groups have had the same experience. Everyone seems to be straining after an elusive phenomenon which is not a real part of anyone's experience. Most of our discussions in that "prayer class" were essentially dishonest. Our dishonesty was grounded in good intentions and was not self-conscious, but it was nonetheless dishonesty. And its effect was paralyzing. We were discussing prayer in terms of what we thought it ought to be, not in terms of what it actually was *for us*. Ironically, most of our texts encouraged us in this. Such dishonesty shows failure to make an adequate distinction between the essence of prayer and the forms we associate with it. And that kind of dishonesty can be jettisoned in the new era when prayer is properly understood as self-offering to the spirit who is God. The above illustration does not imply that real and dynamic things do not happen in groups that pray together, particularly small and relatively homogeneous groups. But in my experience, the success of such groups has usually been directly proportionate to their freedom from established forms. It is also probably related more to their responsiveness to one another and the Spirit in their midst, than to any belief in a God "out there." [13]

THE PROBLEM OF DISCIPLINE

Prayer and worship are forms of religious discipline. They are self-conscious expressions of the life of faith. We have now broadened the definitions of prayer and worship to include the un-self-conscious, unintentional dimension. This reclaims the ways in which men inadvertently pray and worship. And that is needed in an age when prayer and worship have often been limited to particular forms. At the same time, there is a dimension of self-conscious discipline to much authentic prayer and worship.

The problem with speaking of religious discipline today is that the phrase has been ruined. It has come to designate things one has to do in order to be religious. Where no adequate distinction is made between religion and faith, this means things to do in order to be a man of faith. The elements of compulsion and unpleasantness have been highlighted to the impoverishment of the richer connotation of religious discipline. This is because religious discipline has often been *imposed* in a way which denies that it is an expression of faith.

Discipline means discipleship. Therein lies a clue to its religious meaning. A disciple is a follower. Discipleship is follow-ship. Discipline is "discipling," following that (Him) to which (Whom) one is committed. Where God is spirit, the discipline of faith means following that spirit. Since following is usually self-conscious, discipline implies self-consciousness and intention.

Self-consciousness and intention are inevitable where faith is a conscious style of life, as in any identifiable religious tradition. Hence, prayer and worship can be forms of religious discipline. They are practiced by men of faith with some regularity as expressions of their follow-ship. This does not mean that such disciplines always reflect a genuine faith-response. One can follow disciplines of prayer and worship in response to nothing greater than a spirit of social conformity. Neither will disciplines of prayer and worship *achieve* faith, as is sometimes taught. (Prayer is sometimes commended from pulpits as a way of becoming more religious or finding a faith. Preachers who engage in such salesmanship betray that they have no genuine prayer lives of their own.) One can only say that acts of religious discipline *can be* expressions of faith. Such a recognition redeems religious discipline from its identification with that which is unpleasant. And it reaffirms that no particular form of religious discipline is essential to faith.

Thus, disciplines of prayer and worship cannot be made *sine qua non* earmarks of the life of faith. Those who teach that in order to follow the Christian faith you must say your prayers regularly, go to church every Sunday, or receive the sacrament once a year, are simply wrong. A spirit-centered theology recognizes that no discipline is absolute in and of itself, and that there may be faithful reasons for refusing to follow any or all of the above disciplines. However, these same disciplines can be expressive of the faith of many men. (Significantly, those for whom such disciplines are genuinely expressive will not try to impose them on others.) For such men, prayer and worship as disciplines are the leaven in faith's life-style. Because of them, all of life has more flavor and substance. They serve to heighten the self-consciousness of faith in all situations. Because some people pray regularly, they also recognize the prayerful dimension in all they do. For some who worship regularly, even in apparently archaic forms, all of life is infused with a sense of worship. And they become more aware of their un-self-conscious modes of worship.

But this does not justify the imposition of disciplines of prayer and worship on people because it is "good for them." The prayerful dimension of life can be recognized without benefit of anything which remotely resembles a disciplined prayer life. Indeed, for some it comes through a disciplined refusal to engage in any religious practices which seem meaningless. Likewise, an understanding of the worshipful dimension of life has involved for me only such a discipline of worship as is inescapable for an ordained priest. It has probably come in spite of this experience, rather than through it. But our own experience should not blind us to the functions of certain disciplines for others who share our faith. Indeed, for those of us who eschew formal prayer and worship as religious disciplines, other religious disciplines probably take their place. For example, one may regularly engage in social service as an expression of his faith. One may follow family rituals, such as Bible reading or discussions of values or dinnertime liturgies. These can be self-conscious expressions of faith which serve to heighten awareness. One might even set aside a time of day to be (in spirit as well as body) with his wife or children, because this is for him an important expression of his response to the Spirit.

To say this is to recognize that there is a spirit as well as a form of discipline. Discipleship is inseparable from a Christian style of life because the style itself is defined in terms of "following" the Spirit. Any particular form of "discipline" is relative to the style and the context of the disciple. Hence, prayer and worship are not necessarily *the* essential disciplines. But, for some, they can be and often are.

A PERSONAL NOTE

Putting together the thoughts of this chapter has moved me to ponder once again the role of prayer and worship in my own life-style. The illustrations cited above should make it clear that prayer and worship have become meaningful parts of my style only insofar as I have been able to redefine them phenomenologically. When the phenomenon is restricted to particular forms, it becomes dead for me. It loses its spirit.

Still, I am an ordained clergyman and I continue to lead formal worship services. I even find some meaning in this experience. And that meaning informs my style of life. No doubt part of the meaning which I find in worship is a function of my role in it as stage director and theatrical performer. That is personally fulfilling in ways that are part of my life-style, but which may have very little to do with the forms or content of worship itself. Still, the forms and words themselves can take on a special meaning. This is true even of the relatively archaic forms of the prayer book of my own Episcopal Church.

Given my suspicion of noncontemporary forms, and my polemic against rigidity of form, how can this be explained? I believe the answer lies in two psychological phenomena which often occur in worship: association and conditioning.

Worship language and ritual, particularly when it is engaged in repetitiously over an extended period of one's life, tends to take on certain associations. Some of these are very pleasant and heart-warming—even "spiritual." The most obvious illustration is Christmas worship, which for many Christians conjures up associations and childhood memories which have very little to do with the theological substance of the Christmas celebration. In other words, the form and language of worship "triggers" through association certain memories which then make the worship experience more meaningful. This happens regardless of the actual "meaning" of words and ritual acts.

Second, one becomes conditioned through repeated usage to certain meanings. I am aware that there are certain parts of the communion service, for example, which have been reinforced through conditioning for me. These are usually parts of the liturgy with which I at some point in my life had to struggle to find meaning. Or the meaning with which they were originally presented was either meaningless or offensive. For example, to offer "our selves, our souls and bodies, to be a reasonable, holy, and living sacrifice" once struck me as absurd. Now that particular phrase has meaning precisely because I had to struggle to discern what it means *for me*. In effect, I had to make the form contemporary. It is now one of the most meaningful phrases in the liturgy because it summarizes what I understand myself to be doing throughout the service. And this meaning has been reinforced through repeated usage, including occasions when my self-offering had a very specific historical referent and contextual meaning—usually in terms of specific relationships.

I must confess that personal prayer is still a much tougher nut for me to crack. As noted above, in any conventional sense, it is not a significant part of my life-style. For one thing, there is no vocational discipline which forces me to come to grips with prayer in the way that I have been forced to live with and examine my worship. Then too, I have found functional surrogates for prayer in "conversations of imagination." These probably fulfill the same needs as prayer, while being more compatible with my temperament and intellectual biases.

Am I suggesting then that prayer and worship are not significant aspects of the faith which is my style of life? Yes, I am. But that is because prayer and worship are for me largely identified with forms that constrict my God/spirit. Therefore, I can only acknowledge my prayer and worship in terms of discarding those forms (or, at best, sitting loosely to them, as with my worship life) and focusing on activities which more adequately express my Spirit.

6

hoping for today

THE CHRISTIAN FAITH has always included a dimension of hope. Described in metaphors appropriate to each age, the substance of this hope is what makes it all "worthwhile." The Christian hope is what makes a Christian style of life worth the price it demands. This is why hope is as inseparable from faith as charity in the famous Pauline saying.[1] To speak of faith in a Christian context without also speaking of hope is as incomplete as to speak of faith without also speaking of love. Consequently, a relevant faith must articulate its own hope.

What then is the Christian hope? How is it interpreted when God is understood as spirit? What is the substance of that hope for modern man?

We have seen that there is a sense in which the Christian hope *is* eternal life (Chapter 1). The distinction between the two should not be drawn too sharply. But this still begs the question of the substance of Christian hope for our time. To interpret eternal life in terms of the present raises the question of the earmarks of eternal life. What specifically does one experience which makes faith hopeful?

There are at least three earmarks of the Christian hope for modern man: (1) the meaning found in commitment, (2) the joy found in self-affirmation, and (3) the reward which is found in service (or which *is* service).

These three—meaning, joy, service—are also "tastes" of eternal

134

life for modern man. To examine the Christian hope is also, therefore, to discuss eternal life. Hoping *for today* is *the* mark of "living
in the now." This brings our discussion full cycle.

COMMITMENT AND THE SEARCH FOR MEANING

It has become a cliché to speak of the preoccupation of modern
man with the meaning of his life. Actually, man has probably always
been engaged in a search for the meaning of his existence. That is a
function of the self-transcendence which makes him human. It
distinguishes him from the rest of the animal world. What distinguishes twentieth-century man is not the search itself but its self-
consciousness. *Meaning* has come to have a special mystique for
him. Modern man talks more about the threat of meaninglessness,
the gnawing fear that perhaps nothing, including himself, really
matters. This awareness has been sharpened in recent years by the
shrinking of man's world, the possibility of the annihilation of the
human race, and the progressive removal of a mysterious sense of
the unknown.

This is revealed in contemporary literature where meaning is a
prominent motif. Novels portray man's search for meaning or his
despair in the face of its absence. The works of classical existentialists
like Camus, Sartre, Kafka, and Dostoevski are filled with this theme.
The Stranger [2] is a brutal portrayal of the meaninglessness of one
man's life, carried almost to the point of celebration, and the paradoxical emergence of meaning from meaninglessness. In *The Trial,* [3]
the whole structure of justice becomes a symptom of the meaninglessness of life for modern man. Saul Bellow's *Herzog* [4] writes
rambling and poignant letters expressing his deepest personal feelings
because he lacks a meaningful personal relationship. In *The Rector
of Justin* [5] Louis Auchincloss presents a hero whose life is filled
with a meaning born of dedication; but he is undone by the recognition that his ultimate value is an illusion. It has no meaning.
Truman Capote has made a best seller out of the intricate meanings
lurking behind an apparently meaningless murder. [6] Joseph Heller's
Catch 22 [7] portrays the meaninglessness of war, and ends with a
triumphant act of absurdity.

Likewise, in healing the soul of modern man, the theme of
meaning has become prominent. "Existential" psychoanalysis [8] is

more concerned with the meaning a patient finds in his life today than with the reenactment of yesterday's traumas. The goal of such therapy is a life charged with its own meaning and purpose, rather than simply relieved of its tensions and conflict. Viktor Frankl [9] has initiated a school of therapy which sees healing in the light of the ultimate meaning of one's life. The process of therapy becomes the self-conscious pursuit of meaning. And Frankl came to his insights through a concentration camp experience; the usual foci of meaning (vocation, a love relationship) were stripped from him. Carl Rogers reports that his patients experience themselves as fuller persons when they discover their own worth, and find that the discovery gives new meaning to their lives. [10]

The current "ferment in the Church" represents a search for meaning within the traditional forms of Christianity. *Irrelevance* is the major charge hurled at the religious establishment. To say that a particular practice or belief is irrelevant is to say that it is meaningless. It is not related. It has no *meaningful* point of contact with life. It does not touch the real concerns of real people in a real world. Future historians of the Church may view the "new reformation" as a rediscovery of the meaning which faith gives to life, a renewal of the "hope" dimension of faith.

Nowhere is a preoccupation with meaning more prominent than in the vocational dilemma of young people. [11] This is particularly evident among college students. This search for a meaningful vocation is really a dilemma for all modern men, young and old. It manifests itself more clearly among students only because they still *appear* to have some choice in the matter of their "work," the "call" to which they will respond. For most of us, the choice becomes narrowed with each passing year. And in defense against meaninglessness, we push the dilemma further from consciousness, so that it appears less a dilemma.

A central plea of today's student is for something meaningful to do with his life. He articulates this in many ways, in actions as well as in words. One sees it in the radical idealism of some students. This is at the root of most student involvement in political action movements. Involvement is a way of saying: At least in this cause I am serving an ideal which is true and good and meaningful. It therefore gives meaning to my life. The same involvements also say: The structures of society delivered to me are meaningless; the only meaning they yield is found in attacking and reforming them. Where involvement yields meaning, it also yields a sense of vocation. A society struggling for its own meaning should not be surprised when its young people find fulfillment in political action and reform. It should also be cautious in labeling political dissent *subversive*. Such epithets are not only inaccurate, but also meaningless to many young people. Student involvement in political action in our time (on or off campus) usually expresses a vocation for a new and better society. That this should appear subversive of the status quo is not surprising. But the devious and conspiratorial connotations which the word presently carries misrepresent the *meaning* of student activism.

The initial popularity of the Peace Corps and VISTA [12] programs is another symptom of youth's search for meaning. The appeal of both programs is social service, doing something "worthwhile," something that has meaning. Recruitment literature is couched in just such terms. Advertisements for the Peace Corps offer testimonials like "This is a personal experience," "It helped me get my bearings," "For the first time in my life I felt I was doing something worthwhile," etc. Students who interrupt their formal education to enter these programs commonly complain about the meaninglessness of their education, and speak of the promise of "doing something real." The continued success of our present government service programs will probably depend on their ability to maintain this *meaningful* vocational involvement for participants.

Closely related is student involvement in social service projects concurrent with academic pursuits. An impressive amount of student manpower has in recent years gone into social service work in the "inner city." Tutorial projects have sprung up in most of the major cities of the country, primarily through student initiative and under student supervision. In some cities students have been active in implementing the War on Poverty and have helped to "unionize" the poor to protect their own interests. Or they have been active in political agitation on behalf of the powerless in urban renewal and "model cities" programs. Many students consider such involvement the most meaningful experience of their college years. It has made their education seem worthwhile. Or it has kept them from dropping out of school altogether.

But there are others for whom college does not offer sufficient meaning. They drop out of college for what are essentially vocational reasons. Their ranks seem to be increasing at the present time. And their dropping out has very little to do with their aptitudes. Many of them are among the brightest, the most sensitive, and the most highly motivated young people on our campuses. Their complaint is not that their college experience is too difficult and demanding, but that it is not difficult and demanding enough. It seems unrelated to the real world. It lacks meaning. It doesn't deal with the "real issues." It ignores the "action" of life. And these students want to be "where the action is." That is where the meaning is. The college dropout problem is basically a function of the vocational dilemma of modern man, his search for a meaningful calling for his life. And the problem for dropouts is not so much the lack of a meaningful vocation as that the student vocation does not jibe with his own sense of vocation. It does not hold real meaning for him. Those college administrators who speak glibly of an "apathy syndrome" at the root of student dropouts are only half right. There is apathy. But it is not apathy with life itself. It is apathy with a vocation which seems to separate the student for four crucial years from the real world where meaningful vocations are found, and meaningful things are done.

For the same reasons, the search for meaning underlies much of the student unrest on our campuses today.[13] The "demands" of most student discontent are intended neither to overthrow the structure of the university nor to remake it in the students' image. They are bent rather on the reform of the university in its own image. Actually, the vast majority of student demands are unusually moderate and reasonable. They simply ask their colleges to be today what they claim to be and were chartered to be. They call for colleges becoming more authentic forums of academic freedom and discussion. They seek a greater degree of participatory democracy, including genuine student power in the shaping of academic and social policies. Progress in these directions will involve real change in the life of most colleges. Present forms of curricular life as well as social regulations are often outdated.[14] They are experienced as meaningless by the very people for whom they were designed. Most student reforms point, above all else, toward a more meaningful educational experience.

It is ironic that the Church has been so out of touch with these student vocational concerns and dilemmas. The Church is founded on the sense of idealism and vocation which young people today crave and in many ways demonstrate. The irony is doubled when the Church allies itself with the status quo in decrying the forms which these yearnings take. Then the Church herself shuts off communication with those who are most clearly asking for what the Church at her best has to offer.

That offering is an invitation to commitment. Commitment is not institutional allegiance. Neither is it intellectual submission to doctrines and creeds. Nor does it entail conformity to a particular moral code. Christian commitment does have its institutional, intellectual, and ethical dimensions. But it is only properly understood as *self-giving*. Commitment is giving oneself to a particular cause or ideal so that this self-giving governs one's whole life. Where commitment expresses faith, the self-giving becomes an offering to one's God. It is also *responsive*. One gives one's self in response to receiving in a way that gives one's life special meaning.

One of the great paradoxes of Christian faith is that in such commitment life attains its full meaning. Therefore, commitment is faith's answer to man's search for meaning. This is paradoxical because it tells man that in order to have meaning in his life he must give up his life.[15] In order to find he must lose.[16] In order to receive he must give.[17] In order to be fulfilled he must empty himself.[18] And these polarities refer to no simple cause-and-effect sequence. If this were so, Christianity would be little more than a form of moralism. It would become a system for behaving the right way in order to receive the right rewards. The commitment of a Christian style of life is more complicated. Temporally speaking, it comes both before and after the fact of finding meaning in one's life. The New Testament teaches that he who loses his life will find it. But it also teaches that we love because we were first loved,[19] that we empty ourselves because someone has emptied himself for us. All of the paradoxical New Testament language about the first being last and the last first,[20] about the poor inheriting the kingdom of heaven, [21] and about the exalted role of a servant [22] points in the same direction. It reminds us that real meaning is found in giving up one's self. But it also reminds us that one is called to give up his self because he has already tasted meaning. That is the relationship between commitment and vocation. Christian vocation is the call to commitment which lies in being loved by another. It both presupposes and promises meaningful experience. This is what J. H. Oldham means when he says that "life is commitment." [23]

Such commitment involves what Bonhoeffer calls "the cost of discipleship." [24] The grace of God (the self-giving which is the spirit) is "costly." "Cheap grace" is an illusion. If hope is what makes faith "worthwhile," tho "while" can be extremely costly. Discipleship may demand a man's whole life. In one New Testament passage regarding the finding/losing paradox, Jesus allegedly says "He who does not take his cross and follow me is not worthy of me." [25] In other words, he who shirks the suffering which is the wages of following the Spirit is not worthy of the gift. Immediately before this Jesus has spelled out the cost of discipleship in harsh terms:

> Do not think that I have come to bring peace on earth; I have not come to bring peace but a sword. For I have come to set a man against his father, and a daughter against her mother, and a daughter-in-law against her mother-in-law; and a man's foes will be those of his own household. He who loves father or mother more than me is not worthy of me; and he who loves son or daughter more than me is not worthy of me. . . .

The commitment of faith involves a loyalty which takes precedence over even the dearest human relationships. Paradoxically, it is in those relationships that we often encounter the God of the Bible. But that is all the more reason not to be idolatrous about such relationships. Hence we are warned against making a loved one an object of the faith which is only properly vested in Love itself.

How is this commitment related to eternal life and the removal of the fear of death? What is the relationship between the meaning found in commitment and one's attitude toward his own death?

For the man of faith, death is "overcome" in the experience of eternity now, and he is persuaded that nothing (including death) can separate him from this participation. Consequently, a meaningful life implies a meaningful death. What is terrifying about death is its apparent meaninglessness. This is particularly true when life has no meaning. Death is a threat when it looms as the end of nothing, when it marks the close of a fruitless search for meaning. But where death is the end of something, where it represents the *terminus ad quem* of a life given for something, then death itself has meaning. The anticipation of a meaningful death does not evoke despair. Death can be viewed realistically as simply the end of a life of meaningful service, as the termination of one's enlistment in the legions of Love. (This idiom does not reject the traditional concept of the "communion of saints." It rejects only that interpretation which implies an ongoing life for dead Christians. But the concept is affirmed in its basic meaning. This is a community in spirit which one senses with all men of faith who have gone before him and with all who will come after him.)

Death is only bad news when life is bad news. When life is good news and charged with meaning, then one knows himself to be experiencing the fullness of all things, eternity now. Death can deprive him of nothing, except his life—and he has already given that up. But when the fullness of life is always just around the corner, an unfulfilled promise, then death becomes a terrible threat. It may keep you from getting to your goal. It is at this point that the illusion of an afterlife can be very appealing.

Death is a problem for all of us. But it is particularly an issue for older people. For them, death is temporally closer at hand. And at the same time, meaningful vocational options seem more limited, and energies for giving are often diminished. Is the meaning found in commitment limited to young and energetic people? I do not believe so. Indeed, older people are frequently (although not always) more clear about what their commitments really are, and more able to detect the meaning in small acts of giving. Grandmothers who have had to redefine the meaning of their lives when their own children grew up, can become more sensitive to the meaning of a new role vis-à-vis harassed children and grandchildren. Or they may reinterpret their commitment in terms of a new set of nonfamilial relationships. This too can be an expression of faith in which death is overcome. Where hope becomes tied to a temporally limited vocation like parenthood, it can still be reborn, or the vocation can be redefined and rediscovered.

CELEBRATION OF LIFE IN THE WORLD

Because one dimension of Christian hope is eternal meaning in the present, faith's attitude toward the present is affirmative. This affirmation of the here and now is a second dimension of the Christian hope in our time. It amounts to a celebration of life in the world.[26]

A celebration implies joy. And joy is fundamental to a Christian style of life. A faith which does not manifest joy in life is not genuine, at least within the Christian tradition. It is instead usually some form of intellectual or moral submission to institutional authority. Traditional Christian liturgies are filled with words of joy, although they are often intoned in ways that sound anything but joyful. The Psalter, probably the most primitive liturgical document in the biblical tradition, exudes joy. It affirms man's existence in history as the realm of his service of the biblical God.

Joy, however, is not frivolous. It is not a light-headed carelessness which ignores the need of the world. Joy can include agony over personal limitations and compromises, or the limited conditions of one's life. You cannot preach joy to the physically handicapped, to those in emotional or physical captivity, to the economically deprived —without taking seriously the potential joylessness of their situation. Otherwise, one adds yet another burden: guilt for feeling joyless. But the task remains to find joy where one is and to celebrate life where one is. Otherwise, we are condemned to live forever in the future, always awaiting the joy of escape from conditions which may be inescapable. That is a cruel hope indeed.

Because the joy of faith is grounded in the here and now, it cannot stand aloof from the dynamics of life in the here and now. The man of faith celebrates that life as the realm of his salvation. And one of the ways he celebrates it is by deeply immersing himself in it—in all of its turmoil, frustration, anxiety, and alienation. He celebrates the goodness of the world in spite of itself. He celebrates the essential goodness of life in spite of its existential distortion at a given time and place. This is because he has tasted that goodness. And he knows that life in the here and now is the *only* realm in which one participates in that which is beyond time.

This joy is not self-conscious or studied, except perhaps in its formal liturgical expression. The man of faith does not try to act happy. He is happy. But he is happy in a way that does not deny his existence in the real world. He is happy in a way that involves deep hurt over man's inhumanity to man and the suffering which attends human existence. He is happy in a way that includes the cost of discipleship.

One of the biblical images for this joy is the "peace of God," the *shalom* of the customary Jewish salutation. But even this peace is paradoxical. It is an unpeaceful peace. It is not a euphoric state marked by the absence of tension, conflict, and suffering. The cost of discipleship involves a willingness to bear tension, conflict, and suffering as the wages of faith.

This is not stoicism, whereby one simply resigns himself to suffering. Neither is it asceticism, whereby one transcends the world of which suffering is always a part. It is instead faith, whereby one affirms his suffering as part of life, and then gets on with the business of celebrating life. This is because life alone is the realm not only of suffering and chaos, but also of joy and peace. And faith's style of life affirms that you can't have one without the other.

William Percy understands the paradox of peaceful joy:

> The peace of God, it is no peace
> But strife closed in the sod.
> Yet brethren pray for but one thing
> The marvelous peace of God.[27]

The celebration of life in the world can be expressed in many ways. It can be expressed in words. It can be expressed in works, acts of service. Frequently it is expressed in one's whole bearing and manner, the subtle innuendos of one's response to human situations. This is the real meaning of style. An important expression of this joy is humor. Part of the celebration of life is revealed in laughing at it and oneself. The man of faith is relieved of the burden of taking life in the world too seriously because he takes it so seriously. This humor is also not frivolous. It does not laugh at inappropriate times and places, although its laughter often seems inappropriate to those who do not understand. They are the people who seem ponderously burdened by life precisely because they do not take it seriously enough as the real realm of the eternal. Neither is faith's humor defensive. It is not used as a weapon to keep people from talking about things that really matter. It is not used to keep from celebrating life in the world. The humor which is a fruit of faith need not be defensive about life because life is its ground.

Like the humor to which it gives rise, faith's celebration of life is also contagious. The joy of the Christian style of life can be dangerously catching. This joy is therefore also a form of witness. It spreads to those with whom one comes in contact. It infects them. It can even be a point of entrée for another's response to the biblical God. Genuine celebration of life in the world, *joie de vivre,* a sense of humor, acts of service, may be perceived as an invitation to join in the celebration—whether or not one uses the same religious labels, sings the same songs, reads the same Bible, or recites the same creeds.

A failure to recognize the contagious nature of joy has led to some profound theological confusion concerning the realms of the sacred and the secular.[28] Reflecting otherworldly influences from outside the biblical tradition, this confusion has opened a chasm between these two realms which has deeply infected Christian thought.

Within a spirit-centered theology, the sacred and the secular cannot be separated. The realm of the "secular" (worldly, transient, finite) is precisely the realm in which the "sacred" (transworldly, ultimate, infinite) is encountered. Recent theological thought has been almost unanimous in recognizing this point. Yet the Church continues to behave in otherworldly ways as if the world were somehow (in the words of the Episcopal prayer book) "naughty," [29] and Christians ought to avoid contact with it. This is because it is difficult and demanding to accept the world on its own terms. It can involve pain, suffering, turning the other cheek, walking the extra mile, the risk of one's very being. It can involve risks which run the whole gamut of Bonhoeffer's cost of discipleship. That this road is more steep than most Christians acknowledge is no excuse, however, for escape into otherworldliness or a sacred/secular antagonism. That would deny the Incarnation. The meaning of the Incarnation is, after all, that the eternal spirit is encountered under the conditions of time and space, i.e., in the real world.[30]

Like the gift of meaning, this celebrative dimension of the Christian hope is experienced as both a present reality and a future promise. It is both realized and anticipated. This is true of all the expressions of faith's celebration—joy, peace, humor, involvement. In each case, the promise reaffirms a dimension of faith's experience which is always present. To this extent, it is also always becoming a part of one's past. And this is what a man of faith remembers.

SERVICE AS ITS OWN REWARD

If commitment is faith's answer to man's search for meaning, the mark of commitment in the biblical tradition is service. Insofar as service is rewarding, it constitutes a third demension of faith's hope in our time.

What is the substance of this service? To what specific vocations is the man of faith called? How does he determine what constitutes his service in a given situation?

Within a spirit-centered theology, the form of service is indicated by the form in which the spirit is revealed. The medium of faith then provides the norm by which service is measured. The substance of Christian service is the Spirit itself, i.e., Love. In the Christian tradition, where the personhood of Jesus is *the* medium, the normative form for faith's service is the ministry of Jesus. This is what Paul means when he writes "For to me to live is Christ." [31] But this Love/service will take different forms in differing circumstances. Determining the form of Love's expression is finally up to the individual man of faith. (This is the basis of the "new" morality. Every time the man of faith makes a decision about his service, he becomes a moral agent.) In the Christian tradition, the man of faith does not make this decision in a vacuum. Because the Spirit assumes concrete form, the man of faith has a model. And because Jesus exercised his ministry in the light of the biblical understanding of servanthood,[32] the entire biblical tradition provides guidelines for the form of faith's service.

In what direction do those guidelines point? In both the Old and New Testaments, they point to *the importance of persons.* They emphasize that man *is* his brother's keeper. Responsibility then becomes the ability to respond to the needs of others. This is as clear in the mythology of Genesis [33] as it is in the prophetic outcry of Amos [34] or Jeremiah,[35] as it is in the person-centered acts which characterize the ministry of Jesus. In the biblical understanding, one serves God by serving his fellow man. Persons are always more important than things, rules, or even principles. The person-centered significance of Mary's anointing of Jesus is more important than the ointment itself or its value.[36] It is more important to heal a man in need than to observe the rules governing the sabbath.[37] The principle of equality is irrelevant in the relative rewards of the laborers in the vineyard.[38] In Buber's words,[39] the calling of biblical man is to relate to his fellow man as a Thou, a person, a subject—rather than as a thing, a nonperson, an object. The same distinction might be viewed as relating to another as spirit, rather than simply as form. That is the substance of service in the biblical understanding. One name for it is Love as it is acted out in the ministry of Jesus.

This is why the "imitation of Christ"[40] is an appropriate Christian vocational image. It can, of course, be misconstrued as the "mimicking" of Christ, attempting to copy his behavior as it is recorded in the New Testament. This leads to a new legalism, where what we know of Jesus is substituted for the old law. For example, one must not marry because Jesus did not marry. What the imitation of Christ means instead is a patterning of one's service after the model which he is. It is having "this mind in you, which was also in Christ Jesus."[41]

Except by substituting another abstraction for Love, it is impossible to define the form of faith's service without limiting the freedom of the man of faith. It is, however, possible to give illustrations of the kind of service which Love might demand in a given situation. This is the point of the Sermon on the Mount, which is not a new law, but rather an illustration of what the spirit of the "old" law might demand in any given situation. It is also possible to use synonyms for Love which have special currency at a given time. In an age when depth psychology has given special content to "interpersonal sensitivity," Love's service might be defined in such terms. Love is the kind of person-centered emptying of oneself which characterizes the work of a good psychotherapist. Likewise, in a milieu where *concern* is an expressive concept, Love's service might be called concern for the other person. Love's service is involvement in movements designed to achieve justice for the victims of injustice, relief for the victims of poverty, peace for the victims of war. It might also be the self-giving of lovers to one another, out of *concern* for the other's fulfillment. Likewise, in an age when violence has become almost a style of life, Love's service becomes nonviolence and is illustrated by an unwillingness to retaliate in kind against the perpetrators of violence.

Faith's service then, the ministry of Jesus, the imitation of Christ, the servanthood of Israel, etc., is person-centered. Biblically it is grasped in a "God-centered" frame of reference. But according to a spirit-centered theology, that God is spirit and only becomes concrete in acts of interpersonal love. This again is a paradox—that the service of the God who is spirit means the service of the neighbor who is concrete.

Also paradoxical is the sense in which faith's service is its own reward. This is paradoxical because service involves the cost of discipleship. And that cost is not rewarding in the world's terms. It may involve the loss of possessions; [42] giving one's last coat to a stranger; [43] loss of prestige; [44] rejection by men; [45] loss of position; [46] being the object of mistrust and misunderstanding.[47] It may even involve being accused of being anti-God.[48] Most of all, it may involve the loss of one's life, one's very being. All of this happened, after all, to Jesus, who is the Christian model for service. How then can this service be called a reward? How can it be a dimension of Christian hope? How can service give meaning to life when it may mean the end of life? How can service joyfully affirm a world which persecutes the agents of service?

All of this is possible because service is its own reward. The service of the God of Love does not promise any prizes "later on." It does not bribe one with promises of a return on his investment. Martyrs die willingly not because of the promise of an afterlife, but because they know that this is what they have to do. Their hope is for today. That is the source of their apparent peace—a sense of serving that which is eternal—rather than any reassurance of what is coming afterward. Jesus did not go to the Cross chuckling that he was putting one over on the world. He went to the Cross because that was what his service demanded. And he was confident that nothing done to him could destroy the Spirit he served. Indeed, it appears he sensed that his death would trigger a rebirth of the Spirit in other persons.[49]

Service is its own reward in the same paradoxical sense that the meaning of life is experienced as both present and future. The service of Love is rewarding because of confidence that what one is doing is right, worthwhile, and meaningful. This is a humble confidence. It is not self-righteous in a way that assumes superiority over others or passes judgment on their service. This is because Christian service is measured by a humble model. It entertains the possibility that the servant has "goofed" in his interpretation of what Love demands, or that self-centered considerations have usurped the demands of Love. That is one of the risks the man of faith takes when he acts on his commitments. He might be wrong. But there are no rewards without risks.

Also, service's reward is not always self-conscious in either its enjoyment or its anticipation. Indeed, there are good biblical precedents for not letting your right hand know what your left hand is doing.[50] Such self-consciousness is usually an invitation to self-righteousness. The most rewarding acts of service are probably those that are more or less spontaneous, where one loves—is sensitive, concerned, self-giving—because that is the only thing he can do. In Camus' *The Plague,* the hero ends up simply collecting dead bodies and burying them, an apparently absurd response, but for him the only human thing left to do. This makes Love part of his style of life.

Yet the rewards of service are still part of what the man of faith "looks forward to" on the basis of his faith-experience. And this prompts his desire to continue his life. It is certainly basic to his affirmation of life in the here and now.

SUMMARY

Three basic dimensions of faith's hope in our time, then, are meaning, joy, and service. There are, of course, other dimensions of this hope. A popular image for hope among some Christian humanists is "full humanity." Properly understood, that image touches on all of the dimensions cited here. And when it is used, Jesus is usually viewed as the model or revealer of the fullness of humanity. But meaning, joy, and service comprehend the author's experience and that of others, both within and outside the Christian tradition. More important, they focus on dimensions of life which are real for modern man. Hence, they should put faith's hope in clearer and more realistic, present-oriented perspective. If so, one will recognize the temporal paradox of hope—that it has to do with one's personal present and past, as well as future. And this highlights the relationship between hope and eternal life—that "the substance of things hoped for" [51] transcends time. That is because the substance of things hoped for, like the object of faith, is Spirit.

Thus to discuss hope brings us full cycle. It brings us back to faith—response to the ultimate spirit. Christian faith, Christian morality, the Christian Church, and the Christian hope are all spirit-centered. This is because the biblical God is indissolubly spirit. Faith is a style of life responsive to this Spirit. In that recognition may lie the rediscovery of faith in our time.

A PERSONAL NOTE

It is difficult to discuss the meaning, joy, and service in one's own life without sounding saccharine, sentimental, or self-righteous.

Perhaps it will suffice to say that vocational meaning has been a central thrust of my own faith. What may be more to the point, it has been central to my sense of personal worth. That does not mean that I am always confident of the meaning of what I do. I am not. There are still days when I wake up and wonder if there is any real point to what I am doing. There have been occasions when I have contemplated a change of vocation. There have been others when I wondered if what appeared as meaning in the past and present might not be an illusion. I suspect and expect that those occasions will come again. But one of the things that gets me through them is that subjective sense of realness that some call hope. It gives me confidence that what has been and is, also will be. It also persuades me that the present and the future hold untold possibilities. That is because the past has always been full of surprises.

To be honest, I suppose I would have to confess that this hope is not negotiable. I am not sure that any evidence, no matter how compelling, could persuade me to relinquish or deny it. It is empirical only insofar as it is based on my experience of past and present joy, and the rewards of what a more objective observer would see as trivial and self-serving acts of service.

My hope then is finally based on an immense leap of faith. That leap involves, among other things, embracing a religious tradition into which I was born as an historical accident. That is a very tenuous thing around which to orient one's life. And yet, candidly, I do not have very much choice in this matter. The tradition was delivered to me. Somehow, it "took." It took hold of me, however unorthodox my mode of expressing it.

Finally, what may be most important is that this leap of faith involves trusting my own subjectivity. It means believing my own feelings. And that could be a very dangerous thing to do. Yet here again, I am not sure that I really have any choice.

To trust my feelings, of course, is to leap not into the future or the past—but always more deeply into the present. And that is where this book began.

notes

INTRODUCTION

1. In regard to the intricacies of Trinitarian thinking, St. Augustine espouses the theologically sound principle that to say something, however inadequate, is better than silence.
2. "Once to Every Man and Nation," James Russell Lowell.
3. In a similar vein, Bishop Robinson confesses that there is a line which "runs right through the middle of myself" between "the traditional orthodox supernaturalism in which our faith has been framed and the categories which the 'lay' world ... finds meaningful today." *Honest to God*, Westminster Press, Philadelphia, 1963, p. 8.

CHAPTER 1—LIVING IN THE NOW

1. For example, in Albert Camus' *The Stranger*.
2. These questions are at the heart of the issue which tends to divide academic psychologists into the camps of "experimentalists" and "clinicians." For a good defense of the use of the concept of the "self," see Gordon Allport, *Becoming*, Yale University Press, 1955. For a recent experimentalist critique of the concept, see Ruth Wylie, *The Self Concept*, University of Nebraska Press, Lincoln, 1961.
3. For a fuller treatment of this point, see Allport, *op. cit.*, pp. 36–56.
4. The relationship between *self* and *soul* is recognized in Wilhelm Wundt's bold declaration against the self-psychologies for "a psychology without a soul." For a sensitive treatment of the theological significance of the concept of the self, see Reinhold Niebuhr, *The Self and the Dramas of History*, Scribner's, New York, 1955, and Earl A. Loomis, Jr., *The Self in Pilgrimage*, Harper & Bros., New York, 1960.
5. For a fuller discussion of this aspect of Hebraic thought, see W. Köhler, *Hebrew Man*, and Johannes Pedersen, *Israel*, Vols. I–II, pp. 99–181.

6. See, for example, Romans 8.
7. For fuller discussions of a "holistic" approach to psychology, see Rollo May (ed.), *Existence,* and Kurt Goldstein, *Human Nature in the Light of Psychopathology,* Schocken Books, New York, 1963.
8. The best theoretical exposition of psychosomatic medicine is offered by Dr. W. Flanders Dunbar in her *Mind and Body,* Random House, New York, 1955.
9. For example, John 20:19–29; Luke 24:36–43; Luke 8:49–55; John 11: 17–44.
10. See, for example, Romans 12:3–8; Eph. 4:1–16.
11. In *The Autobiography of Malcolm X,* New York, Grove Press, 1965.
12. William Hamilton suggests that a belief in the objective existence of God can be morally debilitating in the same way. See his *The New Essence of Christianity,* Association Press, New York, 1961.
13. I Sa. 28:9.
14. Luke 24:13–35.
15. This historical focus on the narrative in Acts 2 does not ignore its mythological legendary elements (e.g., the speaking in tongues), or its typological relationship to the myth of the Tower of Babel in Gen. 11:1–9. It simply posits this kind of experience of spirit in community as a "type" for what might have really happened.
16. John 20:19–29.
17. John 20:1–7; Mark 16:1–8.
18. Acts 1:9–11.
19. Matt. 28:1–8; Mark 16:1–8; Luke 24:1–7; John 20:1–7.
20. Roger Lloyd, *The Ferment in the Church,* Morehouse-Barlow, New York, 1964, p. 30.
21. John 5:25.
22. *Concluding Unscientific Postscript,* Princeton University Press, 1941, p. 79.
23. Matt. 3:2.
24. Matt. 12:28.
25. II Cor. 1:22, 5:5; Eph. 1:14.
26. I Cor. 15:54–57.
27. Romans 8:35, 39.
28. See, e.g., Deut. 6:4 ff, Matt. 22:37–40.

CHAPTER 2—DECIDING FOR YOURSELF

1. Paul Tillich makes this point concerning the necessity for moral absolutes well in *My Search for Absolutes,* Simon and Schuster, New York, 1967.
2. This polarity is well illustrated in the New Testament in a comparison of the writings of Paul, where faith is emphasized as the basis of good works, and the response in the Epistle of James, where good works are emphasized as a mark of faith. See esp. James 1:22–27. Of course, both are right.

3. *Christian Morals Today*, Westminster Press, Philadelphia, 1964, p. 11.

4. Deut. 12–26.

5. See *On Becoming a Person*, Houghton Mifflin Co., Boston, 1961, pp. 248–50. For fuller elaboration of this concept, see *Client-Centered Therapy: Its Current Practice, Implications, and Theory*, Houghton Mifflin, Boston, 1951, and Rogers and R. F. Dymond, *Psychotherapy and Personality Change*, University of Chicago Press, 1954, pp. 215–237.

6. E.g., in *The Future of an Illusion* and *Civilization and Its Discontents*.

7. *Op. cit.*

8. See, e.g., *The New York Times*, "The News of the Week in Review," article on the new morality, Sunday July 4, 1965.

9. Gal. 3:24.

10. For a good biblical exposition of the relationship between a spirit-centered theology and a spirit-centered morality, see Romans 8.

11. II Cor. 3:3; Jer. 31:33.

12. In *The Lonely Crowd*, Yale University Press, New Haven, 1950.

13. See, e.g., Romans 5–7.

14. *Systematic Theology*, Vol. I, pp. 83–86.

15. For a good exposition of this tenet of the new morality, see William Stringfellow, *Free in Obedience*, The Seabury Press, New York, 1964.

16. Ep. Joan, vii, 5—"Dilige, et quod vis fac."

17. For other recent statements of the new morality, see Robinson, *Honest to God*, Westminster Press, and *Christian Morals Today;* Paul Lehmann, *Ethics in a Christian Context*, Harper & Row, New York; Joseph Fletcher, *Situation Ethics* and *Moral Responsibility*, Westminster Press.

18. For a well-documented study of the kind of hypocrisy which has evoked a reemergence of the new morality in our time, see John F. Cuber and Peggy B. Harroff, *The Significant Americans: A Study of Sexual Behavior Among the Affluent*, Appleton-Century, New York, 1965. The book is a sociological study of the discrepancy between the monolithic sexual code preached by affluent Americans and their actual sexual practices.

19. Luke 18:9–14.

20. Gal. 4:4–7.

21. For an interesting illustration of the ongoing debate between those who hold positive and negative views of human nature without acknowledging the paradox which unites the two, see Carl Rogers' critique of Reinhold Niebuhr's doctrine of man (with the discussion by Bernard M. Loomer, Walter M. Horton and Hans Hofmann) in *The Nature of Man in Theological and Psychological Perspective* (ed. Simon Doniger), Harper & Row, New York, 1962, Ch. 5.

22. See, e.g., Wood, Frederic C. Jr., "The New Morality: Implications for Learning to Make Decisions," *Religious Education*, Vol. LXII, No. 3, May–June 1967.

23. Gen. 3:1–7.

24. For a more elaborate discussion of this understanding of sin, see Tillich, *Systematic Theology*, University of Chicago Press, Vol. II, especially pp. 44–59.

25. I have often spoken publicly, lectured, and preached on the meaning of the new morality, evoking occasionally some mild consternation but rarely any sharp antagonistic response. However, when a sermon preached at Goucher College on October 25, 1964, applied some of these insights to the realm of sexual ethics, it received widespread national publicity and the old moralists rushed to the fore to heap burning coals of abuse on my head and indict me as nothing less than a perverter of the morals of American youth!

26. *Op. cit.,* pp. 146–50.

27. Luke 12:13–14.

28. Recent attempts to address this question from a theological perspective include Helmut Thielicke, *The Ethics of Sex* (tr. John W. Doberstein), Harper & Row, New York, 1964; Robert Grimm, *Love and Sexuality,* Association Press, New York, 1964; Richard F. Hettlinger, *Living With Sex: The Student's Dilemma,* Seabury Press, New York, 1966; and *Sex, Family, and Society in Theological Focus* (ed. John Charles Wynn), Association Press, New York, 1966. Hettlinger's book offers a particularly good picture of the many facets of the dilemma as it is experienced by the contemporary American college student.

29. See esp. *Totem and Taboo* and *Civilization and Its Discontents.*

30. The reader is directed to the author's *Sex and the New Morality,* Association Press, New York, 1968.

31. For fuller expositions of the biblical understanding of the wholesomeness of sexuality, see Thielicke, *op. cit.,* Ch. I; Grimm, *op. cit.,* Ch. 4; and Pieter de Jong, "Christian Anthropology: A Biblical View of Man," Ch. 3 in *Sex, Family and Society . . . (op. cit.).*

32. For an elaboration of this point of view, see the author's "Sex Within the Created Order," *Theology Today,* October 1965, a reprint with commentary of the sermon cited above.

33. "Letter From Birmingham Jail," *Christian Century,* June 12, 1963.

34. In *Fear and Trembling,* Doubleday Anchor Book, New York, 1941, 30–37.

35. Cf. Matt. 12:1–4; I Sa. 21:1–6; Lev. 24:5–9.

36. Plato, *Apology,* "Crito."

37. *Op. cit.,* pp. 120–33.

38. Plato, *op. cit.*

39. Matt. 5:17.

40. For example, by Leon Uris in *Mila 18.*

CHAPTER 3—BELIEVING IS NOT ENOUGH

1. Paul Tillich makes this point well in *Dynamics of Faith,* Harper and Bros., New York, 1957. See esp. Ch. 11, "What Faith Is Not."

2. These are words to which Tillich, more than any other single thinker in our time, has given theological currency. I am indebted to him in my use of them here, as well as throughout the book.

3. Cf. Exodus 19 and 20.

4. *Op. cit.*

5. Cf. *Totem and Taboo, Moses and Monotheism,* and other works.

6. For a more elaborate and scholarly treatment of this controversial point, see Rudolph Bultmann's *Jesus Christ and Mythology* (Scribner's, New York, 1956), and Schubert Ogden's *Christ Without Myth* (Harper & Row, New York, 1961). Some have noted a similarity between my views on this subject and those articulated by David Friedrich Strauss in the early nineteenth century. Although I bear no explicit indebtedness to Strauss on this point, he has exercised a widespread influence on modern theological thought. I find his views in general (and particularly regarding an afterlife, see Ch. 1) compatible with my own. For a good succinct summary, see Albert Schweitzer's treatment of Strauss in Chapters VII–IX, *The Quest of the Historical Jesus,* or Strauss' own *Life of Jesus.*

7. See esp. *Letters and Papers From Prison* (ed. E. Bethge, tr. R. Fuller), Macmillan Co., New York, 1962.

8. For a colorful treatment of this distinction, see William Stringfellow, *op. cit.,* Ch. 1, "The Folly of Religion."

9. E.g., Col. 1:15; Phil. 2:6.

10. The root meaning of *exist* is "to stand out."

11. For a fuller treatment of the concept of "Being itself" as applied to God, see Tillich, *Systematic Theology,* Vol. I, pp. 235 ff.

12. E.g., Thomas J. J. Altizer and Paul Van Buren, and to some extent William Hamilton.

13. *Concluding Unscientific Postscript,* pp. 169–224.

14. See I John 4:7–12 for a clear biblical use of this analogy.

15. Cf. e.g. Matt. 26:57–68; John 8:48–59; John 14:8–11.

16. For a more exhaustive philosophical/theological discussion of God as Spirit, see Tillich, *Systematic Theology,* Vol. III, Part IV.

17. Cf. e.g. Gen. 1:2; John 4:24; Acts 2:4.

18. For a more extended discussion of the relationship between the human experience of spirit and the theological concept of Spirit, see Arnold Come, *Human Spirit and Holy Spirit,* Westminster Press, Philadelphia, 1959. For a provocative recent discussion of the relationship between a theological understanding of spirit and evolutionary thinking in the physical sciences, see Eric Rust, *Science and Faith,* Oxford University Press, New York, 1967 (esp. Ch. IV).

19. See, e.g., *op. cit.,* Ch. X, "The Trinity."

20. A similar suggestion is made by Henry Pitney Van Dusen in his *Spirit, Son, and Father,* Scribner's, New York, 1958.

21. B. R. Nanda's biography, *Mahatma Gandhi* (Barron's Educational Series, Inc., Woodbury, N. Y., 1958), makes good Christian devotional reading.

22. E.g., in the Offices of Instruction in the Episcopal *Book of Common Prayer,* p. 292.

23. *Philosophical Fragments* (tr. David Swenson, Princeton University Press, 1936), pp. 29–43.

24. Mark 10:18.

CHAPTER 4—BEING IN COMMUNITY

1. *The New Reformation?*, Westminster Press, Philadelphia, 1965, pp. 32–38.
2. This is apparently the central point of Harvey Cox's book (*op. cit.*), and its fundamental contribution to the present debate concerning the role of the Church.
3. *Honest to God*, p. 124.
4. *Systematic Theology*, Vol. III, pp. 243 245.
5. E.g., Erik Erikson, *Young Man Luther*, W. W. Norton, New York, 1958.
6. Tr. Walter Lowrie, Beacon Press Paperback, Boston, 1956.
7. See, e.g., *Authority and the Individual*, Beacon Press, Boston, 1960.
8. Meridian Books, New York, 1957.
9. Peter Berger raises all the right questions concerning this possibility in his *The Precarious Vision*, Doubleday, New York, 1961.
10. From the Greek *hieros*—priest.
11. E.g., in an official "Proposal for a Non-stipendiary Clergy" of a group of Episcopal bishops, priests, and laymen. Obtainable from the National Council of the Episcopal Church, 815 Second Avenue, New York, New York.
12. Scribner's, New York, 1960.
13. For a fuller treatment of this relationship, see Tillich's excellent volume *Love, Power, and Justice*, Oxford University Press, New York, 1960.
14. See Luke 6:20–31 for a radical call for social upheaval in the face of injustice.
15. Cox makes a similar suggestion concerning the mission of the Church to his "secular city," notably that it is to call the city more fully to be a city (*op. cit.*, Ch. 5–7).
16. First formulated by Augustine in *The City of God*, Book I, Ch. 35.
17. E.g., Cox (*op. cit.*, p. 235).
18. E.g., Robinson in *The New Reformation*, p. 47.
19. For sensitive and fuller documentation of some of these tendencies within the Church, see Berton, *op. cit.*, Stringfellow, *A Private and Public Faith*, Eerdmans Publishing Co.; Berger, *The Noise of Solemn Assemblies*, Doubleday, New York; and Gibson Winter, *The Suburban Captivity of the Churches*.

CHAPTER 5—DOING RELIGIOUS THINGS

1. Bishop Robinson has seriously addressed himself to such questions; in the chapter on "Worldly Holiness" in *Honest to God*, and in his *Liturgy Coming to Life*. A sensitive treatment of some of the issues involved is offered by the Bishop's wife, Ruth Robinson, in Appendix II to *The New Reformation?*, "Spiritual Education in a World Without Religion." The Bishop also discussed liturgy briefly on pp. 82–88 of the same work. Malcolm Boyd is addressing the same problem in much of his creative

activity, reflected in such books as *Are You Running With Me, Jesus?*, Seabury Press, New York, 1966. And there are indications of an emerging concern with prayer and worship among Catholic radicals, particularly in Europe.

2. For a fuller discussion of the internal dynamics of worship and its traditional meanings and usages, see Evelyn Underhill, *Worship*, Harper & Bros., New York, 1937; Dom Gregory Dix, *The Shape of the Liturgy*, Dacre Press, London, 1945; and Massey Shepherd, *The Worship of the Church*, Seabury Press, New York, 1952.

3. The most exhaustive popular treatment of the problem of theological language in our time is Paul Van Buren's *The Secular Meaning of the Gospel, op. cit.*

4. For this analogy with the language of poetry and imagination, I am indebted to Paul Van Buren in unpublished lectures on "The God of Imagination," Goucher College, May 1966.

5. From "The Highwayman," Alfred Noyes.

6. Cf., e.g., Ro. 8:38; Eph. 1:21, 3:10, 6:12; Col. 1:16, 2:10, 2:15.

7. It is a combination of the Greek *laos* (people) and *ergon* (work).

8. John 5:33; 8:32; 14.6; I John 1:8.

9. This is not true of all prayer manuals. One of the better ones, in a traditional vein, is John Coburn's *Prayer and Personal Religion*, Westminster Press, 1965. See also Evelyn Underhill, *Training for the Life of the Spirit;* Samuel H. Miller, *The Life of the Soul;* Douglas Steere, *Work and Contemplation;* and Ann Morrow Lindbergh, *A Gift From the Sea*, Pantheon Books, Inc.

10. Mark 14:36

11. I John 4:7–12.

12. *Honest to God*, Ch. 5, "Worldly Holiness."

13. For the substance of this discussion of prayer and worship, I am indebted to the Church of the Redeemer, Baltimore, Md., for an invitation to present a series of Lenten lectures on this topic in 1966. That invitation provided the challenge to pull together some thoughts which had been germinating in the back of my mind for some time. I am particularly grateful to the participants in the discussions which followed for their candid and helpful responses. Transcripts of the lectures may be obtained by writing to the Church of the Redeemer, 5601 North Charles Street, Baltimore, Maryland.

CHAPTER 6—HOPING FOR TODAY

1. I Cor. 13:13.

2. Albert Camus, tr. Stuart Gilbert, Knopf, New York, 1958.

3. Franz Kafka, tr. Will and Edwin Muir, Knopf, New York, 1956.

4. Viking Press, New York, 1964.

5. Houghton-Mifflin, Boston, 1964.

6. *In Cold Blood*, Random House, New York, 1965.

7. Simon & Schuster, New York, 1961.

8. For a fuller treatment of this approach, see Rollo May's *Existence, op. cit.,* and the writings of Ludwig Binswanger.

9. See expecially *Man's Search for Meaning,* Beacon Press, Boston, 1963.

10. *Op. cit.*

11. For a sensitive discussion of modern youth's search for meaningful "work," see Paul Goodman, *Growing Up Absurd,* Random House, New York.

12. Volunteers in Service to America, a government program. It is also sometimes referred to as a "domestic peace corps."

13. For a brief and thoughtful treatment of some of the inner dynamics of current student unrest, see Edward J. Shoben, Jr., "Students, Stress, and the College Experience," report of the 1965 National Conference on Student Stress under the auspices of the United States National Student Association. Copies available through the national office at 2215 S. Street, N.W., Washington, D. C.

14. This is particularly clear in the social regulations governing women at many leading institutions whose representatives decry a moral "double standard" but support discriminatory restrictions on women which perpetuate that standard.

15. Matt. 16:24–26.

16. Matt. 10:39.

17. Luke 6:34–35.

18. Phil. 2:7.

19. I John 4:10.

20. Matt. 20:16; Matt. 19:30; Luke 13:30; Mark 10:31.

21. Luke 6:20.

22. E.g., Luke 9:48; 22:26–27.

23. *Life Is Commitment,* Association Press, New York, 1959.

24. *The Cost of Discipleship,* tr. R. H. Fuller, Macmillan, New York, 1959.

25. Matt. 10:34–39.

26. Myron B. Bloy, Jr. has sensed this same dimension in Ch. 6, "The Celebration of Life" in his *The Crisis of Cultural Change,* The Seabury Press, New York, 1965. He rightly sees celebration as an important part of a Christian's response to cultural change. In an earlier chapter on "Obstacles to Commitment," he focuses on the attempt to escape the present as a primary obstacle.

27. "They Cast Their Nets in Galilee."

28. For exhaustive treatment of this distinction, see Mircea Eliade, *The Sacred and the Profane,* Harper & Row, New York. This is also one of the central motifs of Harvey Cox's *The Secular City, op. cit.*

29. *The Book of Common Prayer,* p. 540.

30. Kierkegaard calls this *the* paradox of Christianity, of which all its other paradoxical dimensions are simply reflections. *Philosophical Fragments,* Princeton University Press, 1936, pp. 29–43. Except for a few isolated passages, Kierkegaard never showed an appreciation of the Old Testa-

ment. He may have ignored, therefore, that not just Christianity, but all biblical faith, is paradoxical. It always has to do with the eternal in time. Indeed, Christianity is only paradoxical because of its essentially Hebraic roots.

31. Phil. 1:21.
32. Particularly as found in Isaiah 40–66.
33. Gen. 4:9.
34. See, e.g., Amos 8:4–6.
35. See, e.g., Jeremiah 5:20–29.
36. John 12:1–8.
37. John 5:1–18.
38. Matt. 20:1–16.
39. In *I and Thou, op. cit.*
40. From a work of the same title by Thomas a Kempis.
41. Phil. 2:5.
42. Mark 10:17–22.
43. Matt. 5:40.
44. Mark 9:35.
45. Luke 6:22–23.
46. Luke 5:11; Matt. 9:9.
47. Mark 3:21; Luke 4:20–30.
48. Matt. 26:65.
49. Mark 8:31.
50. Matt. 6:3.
51. Hebrews 11:1.